PAUSE

A Working Woman's Guide to being Purposeful,
Productive & Present

Jacqui O'Bree

Copyright © 2018 Jacqui O'Bree.

All rights reserved. No part of this book may be reproduced, stored, or transmitted by any means—whether auditory, graphic, mechanical, or electronic—without written permission of both publisher and author, except in the case of brief excerpts used in critical articles and reviews. Unauthorized reproduction of any part of this work is illegal and is punishable by law.

Contents

Dedication vii

Introduction ix

Is It Time to Press Pause? 1

Pause to Reflect 3

CONFIDENCE – Having the Power to Press Pause 5

How to Build Your Confidence 9

PURPOSE – Pause to Find Direction & Meaning 19

PRODUCTIVITY – Pause to Produce Results 37

PRESENT – Experience the Joy of Pressing Pause 87

Pause for Personal Growth 91

Pause for Yourself 93

Conclusion 95

Resources & Recommended Reading 97

Internet Resources 99

Book Resources & Recommended Reading 101

Dedication

To my mom, for your support, love & encouragement.

To my husband, for your love, and being the best Dad to our girls.

To my girls, my inspiration and my reason to press pause and be present.

Introduction

Are you busy but unproductive?
Are you sacrificing one area of your life to succeed in another?
Are you racing ahead without any direction?
Is your schedule full but your life empty?

Then pause.

A few years ago, I pressed pause. I was in a career that had all the boxes ticked but I was unhappy. I knew there was something more I wanted to do with my life, but I had no idea what it was. After some deliberation, I resigned from my corporate career in marketing. I left my boyfriend and home town, and moved to a new city to "find myself".

It was both the bravest and stupidest thing I have ever done. Brave - because it takes courage to admit that you are unhappy and do something about it. Stupid - because I probably could have done it smarter.

It was a challenging time. I was hoping for an 'Aha' Oprah moment but that didn't happen. Looking back, it was a series of God hints that led me to where I am now. Books, courses and people opened up a world filled with purpose, passion and possibility.

Since then I have become a wife, mother and entrepreneur. I have moved to different cities, travelled to beautiful places, and found a career that I love. I've had the privilege of coaching individuals, speaking at conferences, and facilitating workshops.

It hasn't been easy but it's been meaningful.

Like most working parents, I've found it a challenge having a career and a family. We have more options; more freedom and more information than ever before, but all these options can leave us confused and stressed out.

I realized that I needed to press pause again.

This time the purpose of pressing pause was to write this book and spend time with my young girls, who are growing up too quickly.

This book is a reflection of what I have learnt over the past ten years, and an accumulation of my training and research in professional coaching, neuroscience and personal development.

My hope is that you will discover the inspiration and tools to create a meaningful life and to be purposeful, productive and present in everything you do.

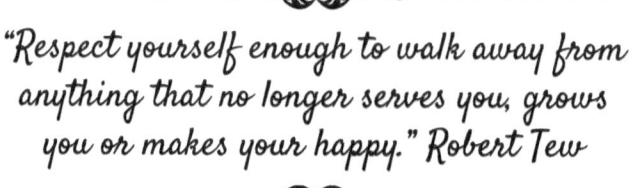

"Respect yourself enough to walk away from anything that no longer serves you, grows you or makes your happy." Robert Tew

Is It Time to Press Pause?

What made you choose this book? What caught your attention?

Was it the title? Could you do with a break?

Was is the idea of purpose? Is your life lacking direction?

Was is being productive? Do you find you're always busy but have very little to show for it at the end of the day?

Was it being present? Do you find yourself rushing through your to-do list and not enjoying life?

The reason I pressed pause the first time was because I was clock watching.

I was sitting in my office, staring at the clock and praying for 5 O' clock. There was nothing wrong with my career. In fact, it was a great career. I had a supportive and inspiring boss. The company was progressive and secure. I earned a good salary and I had just been promoted.

I just couldn't shake the feeling, *is this it?* Am I going to be clock watching for the rest of my life?

Slightly dramatic I know. But I had hoped that my life would be a bit MORE than what it was turning out to be. I could see the path I was going down, and although it was a good path, it did not excite me.

I often refer to that time as my Quarter Life Crisis.

I felt lost and confused for a while, but eventually I found my hands on the steering wheel. Although I wasn't sure where I was going, I was more in control of the path ahead of me. I made choices consciously and felt inspired.

That was 10 years ago, and it's been a meaningful journey ever since. I became a wife and a mother, and found a career that I love.

And I've decided to press pause again. I've been purposeful and productive, but I want to be more present. Clichéd as it may be, but kids grow up so quickly. I am responsible for shaping their lives, and I want to enjoy the process more. The pressures of work and finances, have kept me from enjoying and appreciating this special time in my life and theirs. It's time for me to press pause again, and evaluate what I want, where I am going, and now as a mother, what my children need.

Why do you want to press pause? Are you feeling unfulfilled in your career? Or at home?

"The bad news is that time flies, the good news is that you're the pilot!" Michael Altshuler

Pause to Reflect

Before we start a journey, it's important to know where we are starting from. You chose to read this book for a reason, and before we begin, I would like to share an exercise to help you understand how you are feeling.

The Wheel of Life illustrates the various areas of our life. We are holistic human beings and often, when we neglect an area of our life, we feel out of balance.

Consider each area and based on what that area means to you – and how you currently feel about it – give yourself a score out of 10, marking a dot on the wheel. The score should reflect how you are feeling at the moment, not how you would like it to be.

Now connect the dots.

If this was a real wheel, how smooth would your journey ahead be? Which areas are causing you to stumble? Which areas need attention?

Please bear in mind that there is no perfect picture. 10 out of 10 does not exist!

The purpose of this exercise is to improve your self-awareness, and provide insight into why you're feeling the way that you are. Don't be critical of yourself. Rather use these insights to gently move you to a place where you are feeling more fulfilled.

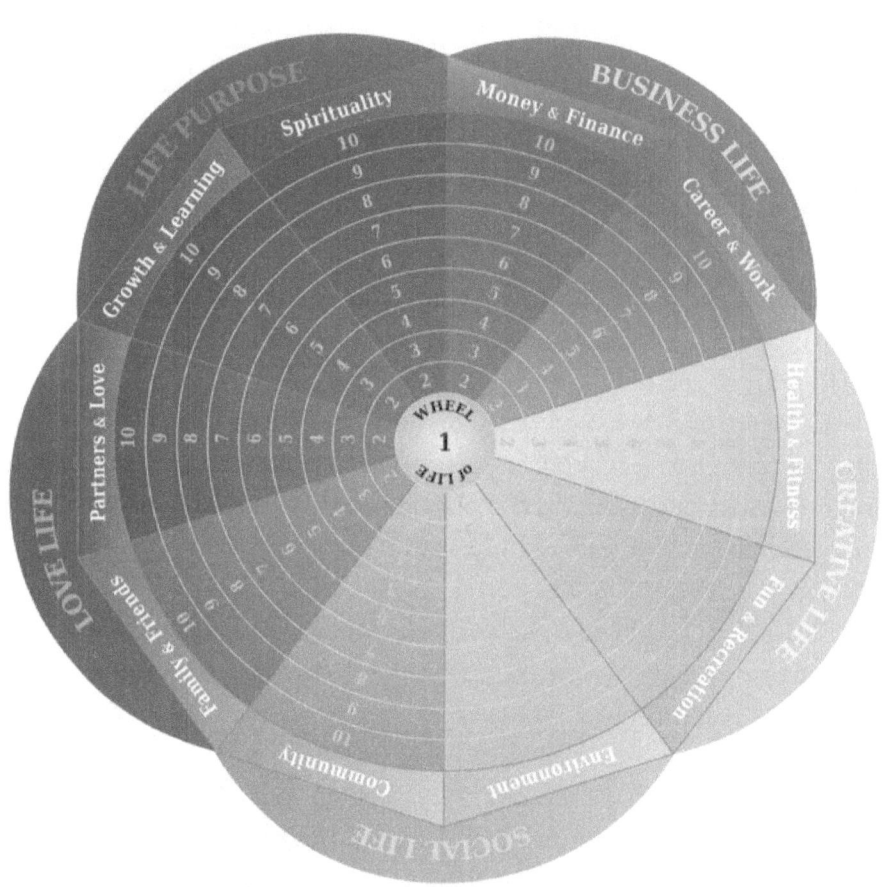

CONFIDENCE – Having the Power to Press Pause

"The hardest battle you will ever have to fight is between who you are now and who you want to be." Author Unknown

Although I felt confident enough to change my career path 10 years ago, I haven't always been confident. I've stopped myself from going after what I want because I didn't believe I was smart enough, qualified enough, pretty enough, good enough, *fill in the blank* enough.

I've realized that confidence is the starting point for most life journeys. If you want to change your career, start a business, or have more fulfilling relationships, you need the confidence to do so.

I've noticed how confidence is often the difference between those who sit on the side lines and those who play the game.

A confident woman pursues her passion. She takes action and doesn't let the fear of failure keep her from trying.

A confident woman stands up for herself and others. She is able to say 'no' to other people's agendas and to time-wasting activities, and 'yes' to who and what really matters.

A confident woman receives (and feeds off) the confidence of others. She is approachable, and people are more likely to promote and help those who believe in themselves.

A confident woman enjoys life. She doesn't take life or herself too seriously.

"When you know yourself, you are empowered. When you accept yourself, you are invincible." Tina Lifford

WHAT IS CONFIDENCE?

There's a scene in the movie *Bridget Jones's Diary*, where Mark Darcy says to Bridget, "I love you… just as you are."

Bridget was speechless. She couldn't understand why Mr. Darcy would love her even though she had messed up yet again, was overweight, and often said inappropriate things. She couldn't understand that he would love her just as she is.

Many of us are like that. We will love ourselves when we are successful, when we are rich, when we are thin, when we are qualified, when we get the promotion…

Confidence is loving ourselves as we are, and accepting who we are – mistakes, flaws and all.

Confidence is often confused with arrogance. Arrogance is thinking you're the best, and treating people as if they are inferior to you. Confidence is the opposite. It's showing yourself and others humility, grace and acceptance.

I'm humble enough to accept that I am not good at everything, and gracious enough to accept that I am good at some things. Confidence is accepting who I am – just as I am. Whether I achieve or not, I am valuable in the eyes of God, and that is enough.

Confidence can be seen. A woman who walks with her shoulders back, maintains eye contact and smiles, comes across as confident. This doesn't necessarily mean that she is confident on the inside. I've put on a brave face when I have felt insecure. Confidence is both an inside and outside job. We can make others believe that we are confident by the way we walk and talk, but lasting confidence comes from a place of acceptance.

How to Build Your Confidence

STEP 1: CREATE A CONFIDENT MINDSET

I watched a short clip featuring the late Steve Jobs, founder of Apple. In it he said, "When you grow up, you get told the world is the way it is, and your life is just to live your life inside the world. Try not to bash into the walls too much. Try to have a nice family life, some fun, and save a little money. That's a very limited life. Life can be much broader, once you discover one simple fact. Everything around you, everything that you call life, was made up by people no smarter than you, and you can change it. You can influence it… Once you learn that you'll never be the same again."

These few sentences demonstrated the power of a confident mindset. What set Steve Jobs apart was not his intellectual ability, but his confidence. He believed he could change the world, and he did.

Confident people don't have much in common. They look different, and come from different upbringings, cultures and nationalities. They like different things, have different education backgrounds and have different financial statuses.

The only thing that confident people have in common is that they *think* differently from others. Confident people have a confident mindset.

Have you paused to think about your thinking? What is your mindset? What do you believe?

"A man is a product of his thoughts. What he thinks, he becomes." Gandhi

A thought or belief is merely a sense of certainty about something or someone. It is neither true nor false. It's a way of understanding things, people, places, circumstances and situations based on our structure of interpretation. This way of interpreting the world has been created by our upbringing, parents, peers, education, social status, culture, nationality, age, gender, religion and values.

"We don't see things as they are, we see things as we are." Anais Nin

If we want to change anything in life, we need to start with our beliefs – as our beliefs about who we are and what we can be, determine what we will be. Our thoughts determine our actions, which determine our results.

For example, if I *believe* I am not clever enough for a promotion, then I won't apply for it and I will stay in my current career.

If I *believe* that what I say doesn't matter, then I won't speak up in the boardroom and I will be frustrated in my career.

If I *believe* that taking care of my health is not a priority, then I won't make time to exercise and prepare healthy meals, and I could end up overweight, tired or worse, ill.

Our mindset, which is made up of our thinking and our beliefs, lays the foundation for our self-confidence. To improve our confidence, we need to improve our thinking. Creating a confident mindset – a new or improved way of thinking – is essential.

> *"Neuroplasticity by definition means the brain is malleable and adaptable, changing moment by moment of every day. We can change the physical nature of our brain through our thinking and choosing. As we consciously direct our thinking, we can wire out toxic patterns of thinking and replace them with healthy thoughts." Switch on Your Brain, Dr Caroline Leaf, 2013*

The way we think has been influenced by many people, circumstances and experiences – but neuroplasticity proves that we can change our thinking.

HOW TO CHANGE THE WAY WE THINK

As neuroplasticity has proven we are able to change our thought patterns, and it starts with a decision to change. Make a decision today to examine your thinking; let go of thinking that is holding you back; and choose thoughts that will empower you.

"Our decisions, not our conditions, determine our destiny." Tony Robbins

Cross-examine Your Thinking. I love watching TV shows like *The Good Wife* and *The Practice*. I love how the lawyer cross-examines the guilty guy, cornering him until he can't deny the truth!

When last have you cross-examined your thinking? We need to be more ruthless with our thinking. Don't accept every thought that comes into your mind. Cross-examine its purpose; its reason for being there.

If it's there to help you, listen. If there is something you need to learn, examine and understand the lesson. But if the thought makes you feel bad about yourself yet again – dismiss it from the courtroom of your mind!

Let Go. You may have thoughts from the past – reminders of the mistakes you have made or decisions you regret. To create a confident mindset, you need to let go of any thoughts or beliefs that are holding you back from moving forward. It's not about denial. You are not denying that those mistakes happened. It's about the decision you have made to move forward. Your decision to be purposeful, productive and present.

I have failed and made mistakes, but I still have a confident mindset. No one is perfect. We have all made mistakes. Confidence is NOT perfection. Confidence is being able to acknowledge your strengths as well as your imperfections.

I once did a very useful exercise to let go of beliefs that were holding me back and it helped me so much that I would like to share this exercise. On a scrap piece of paper write down all your mistakes and regrets, and the beliefs they created in your life. Read them, and ask yourself some key questions. What have you learnt from these mistakes? How have these mistakes served you? How would you do things differently today? Now examine the beliefs. Are they true today? Do they embody who you are right now? Do they sum up how you want to be?

Now – the powerful part – tear up the piece of paper into tiny pieces and throw it away. By doing this, you are acknowledging a new chapter in your life. You have learnt from those mistakes and you are no longer holding onto those beliefs. You are moving forward. Every time you receive a reminder – a thought that comes into your mind about a past mistake – remind yourself that you tore it up, threw it away and it is no longer in your life.

Focus on the Positive. One of the easiest ways to be confident is to be positive. Positive people focus on what is going well in their life. They focus on their successes and don't dwell on their failures. They look for the bright side in any situation.

I'm not saying we must adopt a Pollyanna attitude - where every day is filled with rainbows and sunny skies. That is not reality. We live in a crazy world. There is beauty, but there is also ugliness. There is indescribable joy, but there is also immense sadness. A confident person understands this, and CHOOSE to focus on what is good rather that what is bad.

Be Patient. Thinking is a habitual way of looking at the world. This habit was created over time, and it will take a while to create a new way of thinking. Don't give up. Be patient with yourself and you will notice a difference.

Create an affirmation. A positive statement said repeatedly to counteract a negative belief, which becomes a natural part of the way you think.

Write down a negative or limiting belief that you have become aware of and next to it, write an affirmation that counteracts your limiting belief. Repeat this statement out loud as often as possible. Keep the affirmation short, specific and positive, and use your body to anchor these affirmations by standing tall and confidently.

"Whatever you think about most will grow, because thinking stimulates the genetic expression required to make proteins... If you don't practice it (new thinking), it will not be properly automatized, and it is very possible that your mind will shift back to regrowing that toxic thought." Switch On Your Brain, Dr Caroline Leaf, 2013

STEP 2: BUILD YOUR CONFIDENCE WITH YOUR BODY

The easiest way to boost your confidence in an instant is to change your physiology. I am not talking about losing weight or going for plastic surgery. I am referring to the way you carry yourself.

Observe confident people around you and notice how they carry themselves. Look at their posture, their facial expressions and their body language. Confident people walk with their shoulders back, their chin up and have a warm smile of their face. As a result, they appear approachable and attractive to others.

One of the quickest and easiest ways to build self-confidence is to adopt the physiology of confident people, even when you don't feel it on the inside.

I often present at large conferences. Before I step out on stage I am nervous, and the easiest way to instantly boost my confidence, is to put my shoulders back, look up, take a deep breath and smile.

Many of us know that having a good posture creates a good impression, however, a recent study conducted by Ohio University, showed that not only does body posture affect what others think about us, but also how we think about ourselves. (Source: Science Daily, *Body Posture Affects Confidence In Your Own Thoughts*, Ohio University 2009)

Interestingly, our thoughts are influenced by our posture, and a good posture reinforces the new positive beliefs and affirmations we are adopting. Our brain is constantly checking in with the rest of our body to find out how we're feeling. When our posture is erect, the message our brain gets is 'I feel good about myself', and feeling good about ourselves is the key to confidence.

STEP 3: YOUR ENVIRONMENT MATTERS

I remember as a young girl my mom would often say "Birds of a feather flock together." I only realized later on in life how much of an influence the people I chose to hang around with had on my decisions.

I am not avoiding responsibility, but I cannot deny that if I had surrounded myself with people who had different interests and beliefs, I would have made different decisions. The reality is that it doesn't matter how strong you think you are we are ALL influenced to some degree by our social group and family.

Unfortunately, there are people close to us who hurt our confidence, either intentionally or unintentionally. They say things like, "*You* could never do that", or "Your sister's the clever one" or "Don't think you're better than us". These words are painful to hear and if we hear them too much, we start believing them.

"You are the average of the five people you spend the most time with." Jim Rohn

Your environment matters. Spending time with negative people, or people who constantly criticise you, will influence your confidence. Interact with people who lift you up and want you to succeed.

Following your purpose is not easy. Although it's important to have a reality check once in a while, it's more important to mix with people who believe in you and want you to achieve.

STEP 4: EXPAND YOUR MIND

The story of Roger Bannister and the 4-minute mile was immortalized in the film, *Chariots of Fire*. In the early 1950's, no-one had ever run a mile in under 4 minutes. Doctors and medical scientists deemed it impossible. Roger Bannister, an athlete disappointed with his results in the recent Olympics, believed differently, and was determined to break it. After months of dedicated training, he ran a mile in 3:59.4.

What is incredible about this story is that his record didn't last for very long. Soon afterwards, several athletes broke his record, but it started with one man believing that he could.

More recently Jamaican athlete, Usain Bolt, smashed the impossible. Bolt won the 100m and 200m race in the 2016, 2012 and 2008 Olympics, and holds the record for the men's 100m in 9.58 seconds – something everyone believed was impossible.

To build your confidence, you need to expand your view of yourself and the world. The more you read, and the more you learn, the quicker you will discover that the things that we think are 'impossible', are only because we *believe* they are.

Several years ago, I believed it was 'impossible' for me to run long distances. I had weak knees and didn't believe I could do it. But, there was a part of me that desperately wanted to run. So, one day, I *decided* to run a half marathon.

When I eventually crossed the finish line I was elated. I was so happy to achieve something I never believed I could. Then came the realisation... What other lies had I been telling myself all these years? What else could I have achieved if only I *believed* I could?

Every time we do something we never believed we could, we expand our self-concept and build our confidence. Every time we read a book or watch a movie about someone who has achieved something 'impossible', it expands our idea of what is possible.

Build your confidence by looking at life through a lens of possibility. Find something that you would love to do and start small. If you, like me, want to run, start training for 5kms then 10kms. With each kilometre you run, you will be expanding your idea of what is possible.

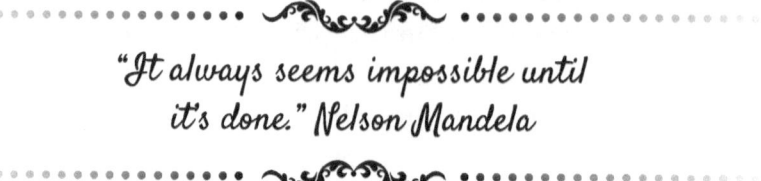

"It always seems impossible until it's done." Nelson Mandela

How to Build Your Confidence - Summary

1. Create a confident mindset by changing the way you think

2. Build your confidence by focusing on your body posture and physiology

3. Manage your environment by surrounding yourself with positive people and people who lift you up

4. Expand your mind by doing things you believed were impossible, reading and learning from others

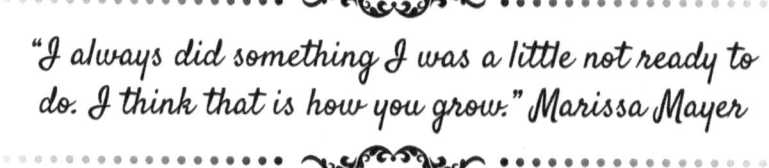

"I always did something I was a little not ready to do. I think that is how you grow." Marissa Mayer

PURPOSE – Pause to Find Direction & Meaning

"The person you will be 5 years from now, depends on what you do today."

During my Quarter Life Crisis, I searched for my purpose. I was under no illusions that I was the next Mother Teresa, Nelson Mandela or Bill Gates, but I knew that there was something more I wanted to do with my life.

It was a challenging time. I was hoping for a booming voice from above to tell me what to do, but that never happened. I read. I studied. I tried different careers. I asked mentors, friends and even strangers for their thoughts, but nothing...

Until one day, while staring out of a window I had a realisation.

Have you ever watched a fly that is stuck behind a window? They keep bashing their head against the glass in an attempt to get outside. Yet if they just flew back a few inches they would realise the window was open.

I was that fly.

I kept bashing my head trying to figure out my purpose, when my purpose was just to live *on* purpose. You might say this is semantics, but when I shifted my thinking from trying to *find* my purpose, to living *on* purpose a whole world opened up to me.

I wasn't intimidated by a grand calling or divine inspiration to do something. It was something far more accessible and achievable, yet still meaningful.

ARE YOU LIVING ON PURPOSE?

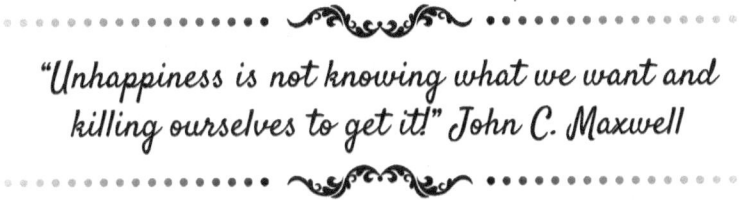

"Unhappiness is not knowing what we want and killing ourselves to get it!" John C. Maxwell

The moment I resigned from my career was the moment I started living consciously. I was no longer living someone else's life; I was living my own.

In coaching we refer to the term unconscious drift. Many people go through life unconsciously. They have no target or destination. They're 'going with the flow', hoping they find fulfilment; chasing someone else's dream; or creating a story of what will make them happy, but this is usually something that the media told them.

To live on purpose, we need to identify our personal values – what is most important to us; play to our strengths, follow our passions, and create a life vision. It doesn't always mean we will achieve it, but doing this makes life more meaningful and fulfilling.

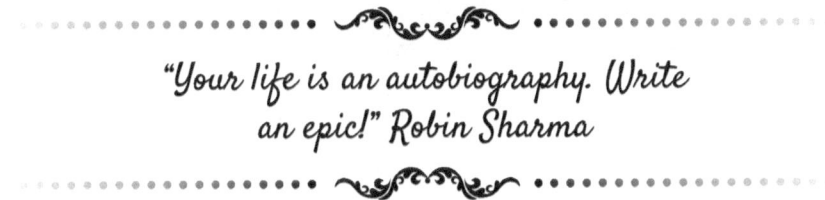

"Your life is an autobiography. Write an epic!" Robin Sharma

STEP 1: IDENTIFY YOUR PERSONAL VALUES

In business, you'll often hear about company's values. They're usually displayed in the entrance hall, boardroom and offices for everyone to see. The company values are the way the company expects you to behave in order to achieve the company vision.

Very few people take the time to consider their personal values. Our personal values are the qualities and behaviours that are important to us. When we do something that goes against our values, we feel bad inside. When someone does something that goes against our values, it upsets us.

Personal values are a measure of what success and fulfilment looks like to you. They're influenced by our beliefs, upbringing, culture, environment, education and experiences. They are unique and can change over time. My values in my twenties are different to my values in my thirties.

People are unhappy when they're not living out their values. It's probably why I was unhappy in my previous career. One of my highest values is making a difference, and I needed a career where I was making a difference in a more tangible way.

By knowing your personal values, you will be able to identify the building blocks of your life vision – what you need to include to create a life of meaning and purpose.

HOW TO IDENTIFY YOUR VALUES

The following is a list of generic values. From the list below identify your top 10 values and rank them in order of importance. The list is not finite. There may be concepts you feel are missing, so please include them.

As you go through the list, you may find that some of your values are similar. For example, if you identify wealth, money and prosperity as important, you could combine them into the word abundance.

Abundance	Energy	Originality
Accountability	Enthusiasm	Passion
Accuracy	Entrepreneurship	Passiveness
Achievement	Equality	Patriotism
Adventure	Excellence	Perfection
Ambition	Excitement	Politeness
Balance	Expertise	Positivity
Beauty	Fairness	Practicality
Being the best	Faith	Professionalism
Belonging	Family-focused	Productivity
Boldness	Fidelity	Prosperity
Bravery	Fitness	Punctuality
Calmness	Focus	Purpose
Cheerfulness	Freedom	Quality
Commitment	Fun	Reliability
Community	Generosity	Respect
Compassion	Grace	Rest
Competitiveness	Growth	Religion
Confidence	Happiness	Safety
Consistency	Hard Work	Security
Contentment	Health	Selflessness
Continuous Improvement	Honesty	Self-reliance

Contribution	Honour	Sensitivity
Control	Humility	Service
Co-operation	Independence	Simplicity
Courtesy	Ingenious	Stability
Creativity	Intelligence	Strength
Daringness	Intuition	Structure
Decisiveness	Joy	Success
Democracy	Justice	Teamwork
Dependability	Kindness	Tenacity
Determination	Leadership	Thoroughness
Diligence	Learning	Thoughtfulness
Discipline	Legacy	Tidiness
Diversity	Love	Timeliness
Dynamism	Loyalty	Trustworthiness
Economy	Making a difference	Understanding
Education	Mastery	Uniqueness
Effectiveness	Money	Unity
Efficiency	Niceness	
Elegance	Novelty	
Empathy	Order	

    Looking at your personal values, are you currently living in a way that represents your highest values? Are you neglecting any of your values? How will you know if you are living out these values? What could you spend more time on? What could you spend less time on? How could you communicate these values to the ones you love? How could you incorporate your values in your career?

    Keep this list close by and assess your values every couple of years. Have they changed? Are you still living in line with your values?

STEP 2: PLAY TO YOUR STRENGTHS

We all have natural strengths and abilities. Playing to your strengths is part of living on purpose. This may seem obvious but often we try to mould ourselves or others into lives that just don't fit.

When I left school, I was encouraged (and chose) to study a business commerce degree, specialising in economics. It's a good degree and a good foundation for any career. The problem was that my best subjects at school were English, History and Art. Looking back, it seems ludicrous that I chose to study something that was pretty much the opposite of what I was good at or interested in.

That is life – we often choose careers or partners based on what other people tell us is good. They are good – just good for them.

Knowing your personal values and playing to your strengths makes the path of purpose that much easier.

Needless to say, I didn't finish that degree and ended up graduating with a bachelor of arts in communication. Something I was naturally good at, and more interested in.

Often, our strengths and passions are aligned. Before you do anything else, make a list of your strengths. If you are unsure of what you are good at, ask yourself what comes naturally to you? What do people always ask you to help with? What do people compliment you on doing? What are you praised for at home and at work? What do you enjoy doing?

Be clear about your strengths and do what you are good at. It's the pathway to least resistance.

But is it important to improve our weaknesses? Oftentimes, yes, but not if those weak areas can be delegated or if those weaknesses are not your core career or business activity. If you are trying to improve your weaknesses, to the detriment of your work and success, you need to question why you are doing them in the first place.

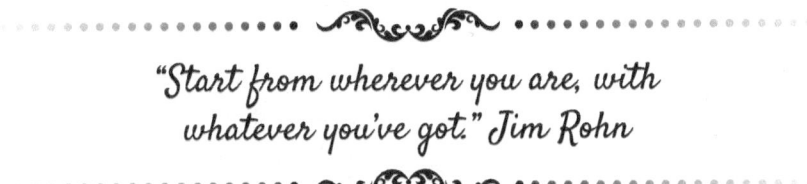

"Start from wherever you are, with whatever you've got." Jim Rohn

STEP 3: FOLLOW YOUR PASSIONS

Find a Career You Love

I used to feel like a "Jacqui of all trades, but master of none". After leaving my corporate career I wasn't sure what I wanted to do. I wasn't born with any outstanding talents and I had many interests. I knew I wanted to be doing something I was passionate about, but I had no idea what that something was.

I started a process of elimination. I compiled a list of everything, and I mean everything, I was interested in, from fashion, to TV production, to photography, to psychology, to e-commerce, the list went on. I listed every career I had ever wanted to do as far back as I could remember.

As my list grew, I researched each area of interest as much as I could. What careers were available? What intrigued me? What was the industry like? What would I be able to do?

From there I set up appointments and phone calls with people who worked in these positions. I was pleasantly surprised by how many people were willing to talk to a complete stranger about their career. By speaking to them, I quickly discovered the good, the bad and the ugly, and it helped me eliminate a few careers from my list.

It was a humbling experience approaching people and admitting that I no idea what I was doing with my life. I managed to put that aside, and focus on what I wanted – a life of purpose and passion.

As my list narrowed I identified the skills and strengths necessary to be successful in those particular careers. I liked the idea of many of them, but based on my strengths, I wasn't suited to all of every career.

We can learn new skills, but we cannot ignore our strengths and talents. When you do things that come naturally to you, you feel in flow. There will always be certain parts of my career that I don't enjoy and that I am not good at, however the majority of what I do is in line with my strengths.

To narrow my search, I created a Love/ Hate list. Although I had quit my previous career, there were aspects of it I did enjoy. I made a list of them, and identified which careers included these aspects. On the other hand, I made a list of everything I really disliked about my previous career, and made sure that my new career would include very few of these tasks.

I imagined my ideal working environment. I am a team player but I prefer working by myself. I love the input of others but prefer to be self-directed. I keep normal working hours; however, I like that my days are flexible. A picture of the environment I would thrive in became clear.

Finally, and most importantly, I looked at these possible careers and compared them to my Personal Values. Which would help me fulfil my highest values? Would any go against my values?

It sounds like a lot of work, but it was a thrilling adventure. The world was filled with possibility, and I eventually found a career that I am passionate about. Living on purpose means following your passions. Not necessarily as a career, but having time for the things that make you feel alive. Don't ignore your passions, while pursuing someone else's passion. Life is too short to live it passion-less.

"If you haven't found what you love to do, keep looking. Don't settle. As with all matters of the heart, you'll know when you find it." Steve Jobs

Before You Quit Your Day Job

Before you quit your day job, I would like to clear two misconceptions. Firstly, there is no perfect career. Loving what you do, doesn't mean that conditions will be perfect. There are many challenges in every career. But loving your career, makes it easier to weather the storms.

Another misconception is that your dream career will find you. Many people complain about their careers, and stay in dead-end jobs hoping their 'dream career' will find them. It won't. If you really dislike your career or feel you should be doing something else, then you need to take action.

Once you make a decision to find a career that you love, be financially prepared, especially if you're starting your own business. Success doesn't happen overnight and you need to cover usual monthly expenses for a couple of months.

If possible, find a new job or part time work before you resign. This will alleviate some of the financial pressure. You may need to make time in the evenings to explore and learn, but the late nights will be worth it in the long term.

Prepare those closest to you and explain to them why you are going on this journey, and what you are hoping to achieve. Believe in yourself, be patient and don't give up. Life is too short to be in a job you hate!

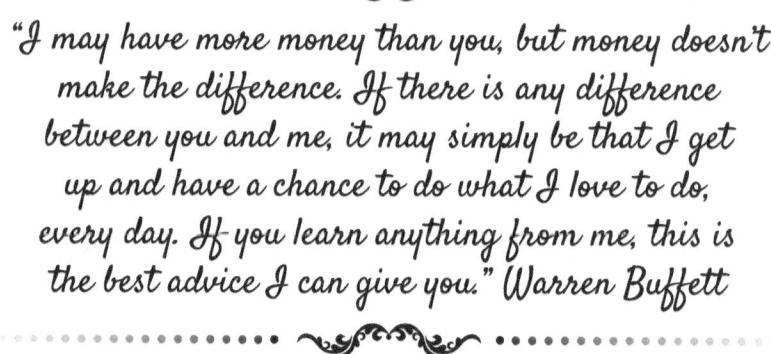

"I may have more money than you, but money doesn't make the difference. If there is any difference between you and me, it may simply be that I get up and have a chance to do what I love to do, every day. If you learn anything from me, this is the best advice I can give you." Warren Buffett

Love the Career You're In

Maybe there was a time when you loved your career, but you feel you have lost your passion. Changing careers is not necessarily the solution. You can learn to love the career you're in by making small adjustments.

One of the reasons we lose our career passion is because we get too caught up in doing work we're not good at. There will be parts of our career that we don't enjoy or we're not that good at, but these parts need to be kept to the minimum. It's difficult to love your career, when you feel like work is difficult. There is always room for improvement, but playing to your strengths makes your career more enjoyable.

Look at your daily tasks or projects that you love, and find more opportunities in your company or team to do them. If these opportunities are limited, ask yourself why you love these tasks or projects. Your reasons will reveal what you could be doing more of.

I love presenting workshops. I love it because it's an opportunity to research and design new material. The process of designing new material is a chance for me to be creative. As I am only able to do a limited number of workshops per month, I need to look for other ways to unleash my creative side.

When people talk about finding more passion, what they're often really looking for is more meaning. Everyone wants to feel that they are making a difference. Connect to your company's purpose and identify how your company and your role in it, is making a difference.

A few years ago, I ran a workshop for a prosthetic company. We had a discussion about loving your career and one of the sales executives approached me afterwards. He was unmotivated and couldn't connect to his company's purpose. He sold prosthetics to surgeons and wasn't inspired by medical technology. I disagreed. He sold prosthetics to the surgeon, but the patient was getting a second chance in life. He was in the business of second chances – now isn't that inspiring!

"Purpose is the Mother of Motivation and Master of Commitment." Myles Munroe

Make Time for Your Passion

If you love your career but it's not your passion, you don't need to resign. Not every career has to be your passion. Often when people quit their jobs to turn their love for something into a career or business, they lose their passion. Not all passions make a profit, but it's important to find fulfilment outside of work.

Make time in your week for your passions. I know as a working parent that this can seem impossible, but a hobby can help relieve stress and energise you. Share your passion with your family. They might not feel the same way about it, but you will be setting a good example of a passionate life.

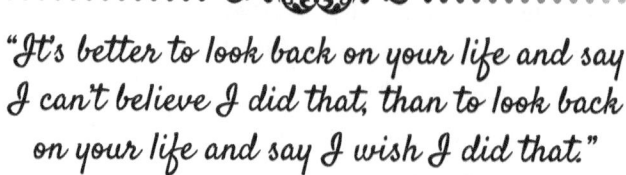

"It's better to look back on your life and say I can't believe I did that, than to look back on your life and say I wish I did that."

STEP 4: CREATE A LIFE VISION

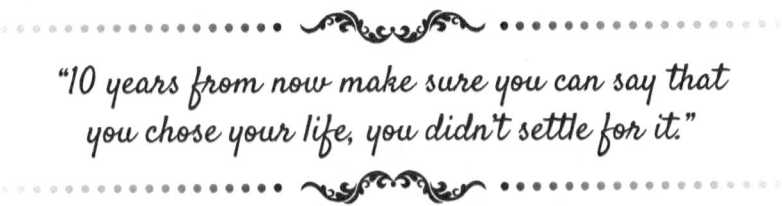

"10 years from now make sure you can say that you chose your life, you didn't settle for it."

A Life Vision is a picture of what you would like to experience, achieve and do in life, and most importantly who you want to become. It gives your life purpose and direction, and keeps you focused on what you need to do in the present... to live the life of your dreams in the future. A life vision helps to prioritise what is important, and enables you to plan and set meaningful goals.

When creating a life vision, include all the areas of your life. We are more than our careers. Unfortunately, there are many people out there who put their careers ahead of their families. At the end of the day, no-one called the office on their deathbed...

Think about what you would like to experience, see, do, have, contribute, discover, learn, or master in your Career (Knowledge, Skills, Achievements, Aspirations, Contributions); your Relationships (Family, Friends, Significant Other); your Health (Physical, Emotional, Mental); and your Wealth (Home, Car, Toys, Hobbies). Describe in as much detail as possible what you would like each area to look like.

Ask powerful questions. What do you want to be remembered for? What would you do if you had more time in the day? What would you do if money was unlimited? What brings you joy? What are you passionate about? What causes are worth fighting for? What do you want more of in your life? What do you want less of? What would you do if success was guaranteed?

If you're visually inspired person, create a vision board – a pictorial representation of your life vision. Gather a collection of magazines, cut out images that inspire you, and create a poster board of your desired life.

A life vision is not just about pretty places and possessions. More importantly it's about who we are along the way. It's how we treat people, and the qualities, characteristics and personal values we live by. It may seem macabre, but think about what you would like people to say about you at your funeral. What do you want your significant other, family, friends and colleagues to say about you?

If the thought of creating a life vision is daunting, break it down into manageable pieces. What do you want your life to look like a year from now, 5 years from now, 10, 20 etc.?

A Life Vision is not a once off project, it evolves as you evolve. Dream big and have fun with it. Remember that your life will never be more than what you make of it.

You may be thinking, what happens if my life vision doesn't go according to plan?

I created a vision for these past 10 years and to be completely honest, it didn't work out how I imagined and wanted it to. However, every step has been meaningful. I have been conscious of what has worked and what hasn't. I'm content with the way it's turned out and I would rather have had a vision and only achieved part of it… than not have had a vision and achieved none of it.

Your Personal Values + Your Strengths + Your Passions + Your Life Vision = Your Purpose

BRING YOUR VISION TO LIFE

"Goals turn the invisible into the visible." Tony Robbins

Having a life vision can be inspiring and daunting. Bring your vision to life by breaking it down into manageable chunks and setting goals. Setting goals is an important time management skill. Goals helps us to prioritise, plan and schedule our days, weeks and months. They also help to bring our vision to life. A vision without goals, will remain a vision.

Think about your life a year from now, and identify three areas you would like to change, enhance or improve.

Don't set yourself up for failure by setting too many goals. Prioritise the most important areas by asking yourself: What would make the biggest difference in my life a year from now?

Set SMART Goals – Specific, Measurable, Attainable, Resonant, Thrilling. Many people confuse goals with wishes. For example, "I want to lose weight" is a wish. "I want to lose 5 kilograms by 1 December" is a goal.

The first step in setting SMART goals is to be SPECIFIC. What exactly do you want to achieve? Describe it in as much details as possible.

Next your goal needs to be MEASURABLE. How much progress or change, and by when? I recommend using a rating system of 1 – 10 for intangible concepts. Rate where you are now, and where you would like to be a year from now.

Next, is your goal ATTAINABLE? If you would like to climb Mount Everest but you haven't climbed Table Mountain, then perhaps Everest is not attainable (yet). A more achievable goal for now, is to climb Table Mountain.

RESONANT – is this a goal *you* really want? Is it in line with your values? Or is it a *should* goal? I believe that the no. 1 reason people don't achieve their goals is because they set goals they don't really want. Their husband suggested it, their friends are all doing it, or their boss thinks it's a good idea. Make sure your goals are something YOU truly want to achieve.

THRILLING – your goal needs to excite you. You want to jump out of bed in the morning in anticipation of achieving it. Don't set boring goals. Identify a goal that inspires you.

To stay motivated, list the reasons why you want to achieve your goal – what is driving you? What are the benefits of achieving this goal? Keep the list close by and read it every time you feel unmotivated.

Now create a plan to achieve your goals. Think about what you need to do and by when. What are the steps you need to take to achieve your goal? How can you can reward yourself along the way? Who is going to support you?

Consider getting an Accountability Partner – someone who will agree to support you, and hold you accountable for meeting deadlines, reaching goals and making progress. It can be a friend, colleague, mentor or a professional life coach.

Another option is to create a Dream Team – a group of five or six people who meet every week or month for the purpose of problem solving, brainstorming, networking, encouraging and motivating each other. It's a powerful way to support your dreams and bring ideas and inspiration to your business and personal life.

"Twenty years from now you will be more disappointed by the things that you didn't do than by the ones you did do." Mark Twain

How to Live on Purpose – Summary

1. Identify and live out your Personal Values

2. Play to your Strengths

3. Follow your Passions

4. Create a Life Vision

5. Set SMART goals to bring your vision to life

"If you're willing to do for a year what others won't, you can live the rest of your life, like others can't." John Assaraf

PRODUCTIVITY – Pause to Produce Results

"Nature doesn't hurry, yet everything is accomplished." Lao Tzu

Not long ago I was busy from the moment I woke up, to the moment I went to bed. I had a lot to do and the list never ended. At the end of day, I wondered, *"Where did the day go?"* I felt frustrated because I didn't have much to show for my busyness. I wasn't getting the results I wanted in my business. I was stressed as a mom, which my kids and husband felt, and I had no time for friends or my health. There was something wrong with this picture.

WHY ARE WE SO BUSY?

Everywhere you go, people are busy. Ask a friend how they are doing, and they reply "busy". I almost feel obliged to say I'm busy, even if I'm not… because If I'm not busy, then what *am* I doing?

These days, being busy and 'juggling it all' has become somewhat of a status symbol. Busy has become a title that we are proud of, but is it a title worth having? Why are we so busy?

I don't recall my grandparents being busy. Yet they still managed to have a pretty good life. Somewhere along the line it's become acceptable, and expected, to be busy.

I read a piece in the New York Times titled *The Busy Trap*. In it, author Tim Kreider, wrote, "Busyness serves as a kind of existential reassurance, a hedge against emptiness; obviously your life cannot possibly be silly or trivial or meaningless if you are so busy, completely booked, in demand every hour of the day… I can't help but wonder whether all this histrionic exhaustion isn't a way of covering up the fact that most of what we do doesn't matter."

It made me think. What was I covering up? I was consumed with making my new business a success but was it really because of financial pressure?

The answer was 'Yes and No'. I needed to make my business a success so I earned a decent salary, but I was also using my busyness to cover up how I was feeling.

As a new mom, relatively new wife, and a new business owner, I felt overwhelmed. My life wasn't going as planned, and I felt vulnerable. It was easier to be busy than address how I was feeling. I didn't want to fail, especially now that I was a mom.

Becoming a mother has been an incredibly humbling experience. I don't want to be too hard on myself. I always do the best I can, but looking back *I know* I hid behind the busyness of work, to avoid how I was feeling. It was easier to sit with the discomfort of building a business, than to sit with the discomfort of being a new mom living in a new city… in a life I hadn't planned.

I received solace from the book *Present Over Perfect* by Shauna Niequist. In it she described her own struggles with motherhood, intimacy, and success. She managed to articulate how I had been feeling, and it was comforting to know that I wasn't alone.

She wrote, "We dive into information or work or bicycling or whatever, because it feels good to be good at something, to master something, to control something when marriage and intimacy often feel profoundly out of our control."

Busyness won't help you to achieve your purpose. If anything, it will make you miss your purpose. Busyness keeps us from being present – with our feelings and with those who matter most.

Reflect on your busyness. Is it helping you to achieve your vision and values? Is it producing the results you desire at home and at work? Is your busyness a cover up for how you are really feeling?

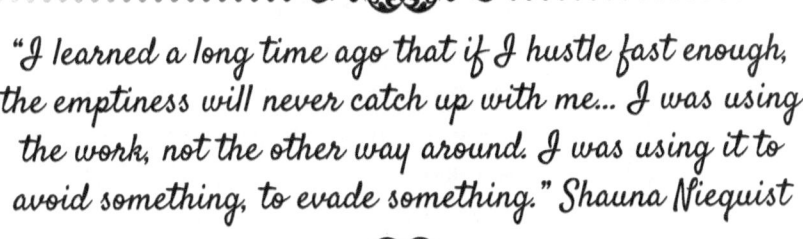

"I learned a long time ago that if I hustle fast enough, the emptiness will never catch up with me... I was using the work, not the other way around. I was using it to avoid something, to evade something." Shauna Niequist

PAUSE FOR PRODUCTIVITY

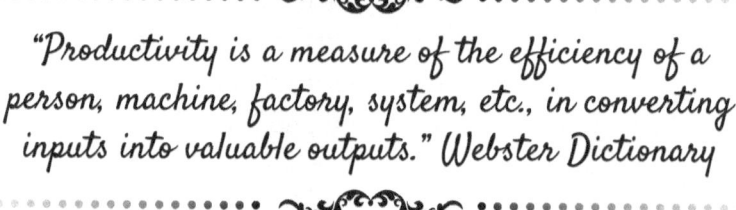

"Productivity is a measure of the efficiency of a person, machine, factory, system, etc., in converting inputs into valuable outputs." Webster Dictionary

If we're going to be spending time away from the ones we love, even if it's on work that we love, we need to be using this time efficiently. I'm a firm believer in working smart, not hard. Being busy is hard. Being productive is smart.

Productivity starts with getting real about *who* is responsible for how we use our time. I remember the first time I heard the term *personal responsibility*. It was both liberating and frightening. I realized that I was responsible for my life, and it was my choice what I did with it.

However, I realized that everything I had or hadn't achieved was my responsibility too. There were circumstances beyond my control, but I still chose how I responded to those circumstances. The level of my achievements, my finances, my health, my relationships were all a result of the decisions I had made.

If we want to change anything in life, we have to take responsibility. We can't blame our circumstances or the people around us. We are responsible for how we use our time, and only we can change it.

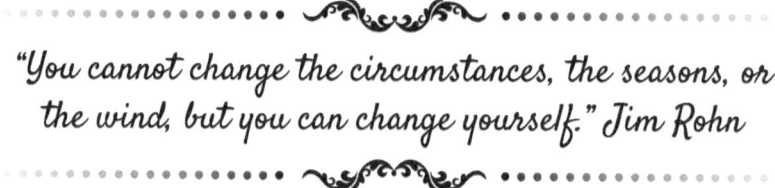

"You cannot change the circumstances, the seasons, or the wind, but you can change yourself." Jim Rohn

TIME MANAGEMENT = SELF-MANAGEMENT

Time management is essentially self-management. If you can manage yourself, you're better able to manage your time, and the distractions and people around you. We are mental, emotional and physical beings. By creating positive habits in these three areas we are able to manage ourselves and our time better.

Mental Management – How to Manage Your Mind

Have you been on diet? A friend of mine lost nine kilograms (20 pounds) on the latest banting diet, so I thought I'd give it a try. I was super motivated the first few weeks and even lost a bit of weight, but by month two, I was raiding the cookie jar quicker than you can say 'No carbs!'

The flaw in wanting to change is that we immediately go into action mode. I want to lose weight; I join the gym. I want to get promoted; I sign up for a leadership course. I want to get rich; I start saving. I want to manage time; I buy a scheduling app.

None of these actions are wrong, but 9 times out of 10, those actions don't last. To create lasting behavioural change, we need to start with our mind. We need to become aware of what is driving our action or lack of action.

Our thinking and what we believe, determines our actions. Whatever we do, started with a thought. If we want to do differently, we need to think differently.

It's Monday morning and an important project lands on your desk. Your boss says he needs it by Wednesday. You think *"I'll do it tomorrow"* and instead check emails, browse social media and catch up on the weekend gossip.

Tuesday comes and something else lands on your desk; this time it's urgent. Your important project has to wait. Wednesday arrives and you spend the entire day trying to finish it. You eventually hand it in the project, knowing you could have been done it better, if only you had more time. This all started with a thought – "*I'll do it tomorrow!*"

Our thinking determines our actions, which determines our results. Someone who thinks there is never enough time, will always feel frazzled and run from errand to errand without ever feeling accomplished.

What do you think about when it comes to time? Do you have any predominant beliefs about time? Is time important to you? Do you believe time is a gift? Do you believe time is money? Do you believe time is irrelevant?

These beliefs are influencing how you use time. Imagine if every time you thought, "I'll do it tomorrow", you replaced it with "Today matters." Would you get different results?

Imagine if your predominant belief about time was "Carpe Diem - Seize the day!" If you believed this, you'd never waste time. Or Nike's slogan, "Just do it". This belief would encourage you to take action immediately.

Think about your thinking. Notice the predominant thoughts or beliefs you have about time. Are they helping you, or are they harming you? Choose a new more empowering belief about time, and notice a change in your behaviour.

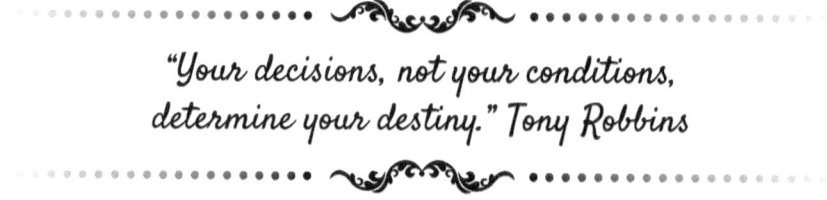

"Your decisions, not your conditions, determine your destiny." Tony Robbins

How to Manage Your Mental State – Summary

1. Think about your thinking

2. Notice your predominant thoughts and beliefs

3. Choose a new more empowering belief and repeat it until it becomes a new way of thinking

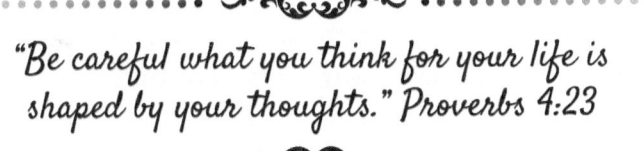

"Be careful what you think for your life is shaped by your thoughts." Proverbs 4:23

EMOTIONAL MANAGEMENT – HOW TO MANAGE YOUR MOOD

We often play victim to our mood. Our mood controls what we do or don't do, what we say or don't say. I just don't feel like it, so I won't do it. I feel angry, so I'll tell him. To manage ourselves we need to learn how to manage our mood. To become its master not its slave.

I am sure we can agree that when it comes to getting things done, it's helpful to feel motivated. When we are motivated, we feel inspired to take action and get things done.

We can't go through life with a motivational speaker attached to our hip, so we need to develop intrinsic motivation. Motivation that comes from within.

There isn't a magic formula for motivation. We need to be practical by planning our day in way that keeps us motivated. Many personal development teachers suggest starting the day with 'An hour of Power'. As a working mom, I am lucky if I get 5 minutes to myself in the morning, so I've got into the habit of getting up an hour earlier than the rest of the family. I use this 'alone time' to read, pray and prepare for the day ahead. I feel more present and focused when I start my day this way.

The way we start the day often predicts the day. Create a positive and inspiring morning routine that works for you. Start your day with purpose by reflecting on your Personal Values, Life Vision and goals. Revisit your Vision Board, and feel the inspiration it provides.

Try not to watch or listen to the news first thing in the morning. It's a terribly depressing way to start your day and can wait until later. Rather play uplifting music, pray, meditate, or journal. If you face traffic or have a long commute, take advantage of this time by listening to podcasts or an audiobook.

One of the best ways to start your day is with 'An Attitude of Gratitude'. Every morning, write a list of at least 10 things you are grateful for. Our attitude plays a large role in managing our motivation. If we live with a bad attitude it's only natural that we will feel unmotivated. Choose a positive attitude each day – an attitude that acknowledges the things we cannot control; does something about the things we can;

focuses on the good; and is grateful (even if it is simply to 'learn the lesson' from a terrible situation).

Routine can be helpful but it can also destroy motivation. Break out of your routine and surprise yourself. Try a new exercise class, find a new way to work, try a different restaurant or cook something exotic. The exhilaration you feel will fuel your motivation.

CHANGE YOUR MOOD IN AN INSTANT

The Change Your State Model by Toby Robbins has been extremely helpful in managing my mood. In his model, Robbins explains that by changing our focus (what we think about), our language (how we talk about a situation) and our physiology (our body and movement), we can change how we feel in an instant.

If I need motivation to go for a run, I start by shifting my focus. Very often when we don't feel like doing something, we're focusing on the negative aspects, instead of the benefits. So instead of focusing on the cold weather, or how tiring it will be; I change my focus to how good I will feel after my run, and how running is making me fitter, stronger and leaner.

The second element of the Change Your State Model is to change the way we speak. Instead of talking about going for a run dread, I say how excited I am to go running, and how great it feels to run. By talking positively about a situation, we send a message to our brain that this is something we want to do, and we build the motivation from the inside.

The final element is to change our physiology. Have you observed a motivated person? They walk quicker, speak with energy and have a confident posture. By modelling their physiology/ behaviour, we send messages to our brain that we are motivated and as a result start to feel it.

"Emotion is created by motion. Everything we feel is a result of how we use our bodies. Identify the physiology linked to a state and you can create the states you desire." Tony Robbins

How to Manage Your Emotional State – Summary

1. Start your day in a positive way

2. Have an attitude of gratitude by listing what you grateful for

3. Break out of your routine

4. Change how you feel in an instant by changing your focus, your language and your physiology

"People often say that motivation doesn't last. Well, neither does bathing – that's why we recommend it daily." Zig Ziglar

PHYSICAL MANAGEMENT – HAVING THE ENERGY TO GET THINGS DONE

I often refer to energy as the secret ingredient of successful time management. We love focusing on to-do lists and scheduling, but the truth is, if we don't have energy, we can't get through our to-do list or meet our schedule. Energy is essential to get through the day.

A lack of energy can impact our productivity, while abundant energy helps us get results quickly and easily. Our energy levels are affected by numerous things: what we eat and drink, how much we sleep and exercise, and our emotional well-being.

If we want more energy, we need to eat for energy. According to researchers, employees with a poor diet are 66% less productive than their colleagues who regularly eat whole grains, fruit and vegetables.

A few years ago, two things largely dictated my food choices: dishes and ingredients that I believed wouldn't make me fat, or that would give me comfort. Of course, these two choices worked against each other, and I battled with my weight and energy levels for many years.

It was only after I changed my focus that my weight and energy started to change. Instead of seeing food as comfort or a source of fat, I started seeing food as fuel. I started asking myself a few questions. What will nourish me? What will give me energy? As a result, I lost weight and my energy sky rocketed.

I am not a dietitian and there is no 'one size fits all' approach. These are the healthy eating habits that have helped me.

I always start my day with a cup of hot water and a slice of lemon. Hot lemon water boosts your immune system, balances your PH levels, aids digestion, clears skin and hydrates your body. Later in the morning, I like to drink a fresh juice, preferably green. Green juices are filled with antioxidants and don't have as much sugar as regular fruit juices.

I try not to skip meals because I end up overeating (mostly the wrong types of food) later in the day. I aim for three healthy meals that consist of food that is low in sugar, high in protein and low in processed carbohydrates. I have healthy snacks in my hand bag, car and desk. Nuts and fruit are my best choice for an afternoon energy fix.

I've always loved water and drink loads of it. Water hydrates the body, increases energy, promotes weight loss, flushes out toxins, improves skin complexion, is a natural headache remedy, and puts you in a good mood. There are so many benefits – just start, you won't regret it!

The next step to boosting your energy is getting quality sleep. Researchers have discovered that sleep deprivation costs business an estimated $63 billion per year.

A lack of sleep impacts our productivity, and technology is not helping. Scientific studies have shown that looking at our phones in bed makes it harder to fall and stay asleep.

"Our bodies naturally follow a cycle that helps us stay awake and alert during the day and helps us get rest at night. But when we look at our screens as we're getting ready for sleep, our brains get confused. That light has a similar effect to the sight of the morning sun, which causes the brain to stop producing melatonin, a hormone that gives your body "time to sleep" cues. By disrupting melatonin production, smartphone light can disrupt your sleep cycle." (Source: Business Insider, *How Smartphone Light Affects Your Brain And Body*; by Kevin Loria and Skye Gould)

Arianna Huffington, founder of the Huffington Post, is so passionate about this subject, that she wrote a book called *The Sleep Revolution*. After she collapsed from exhaustion in 2007, she has been on a mission to educate the public about the importance of sleep.

There is a myth that we can do our jobs well on four or five hours of sleep a night. But research has shown that our cognitive functions are impaired, so we are more likely to overreact. Our emotional intelligence is degraded, so we are more likely to be irritable, and sleep deprivation has been linked to mental health problems and depression. (Source: Fast Company, *Here's Arianna Huffington's Recipe for a Great Night of Sleep*, Rina Raphael)

Whether you're a night owl or an early bird, it doesn't matter. It's not the number of hours you sleep, but rather the quality of your sleep, that matters most. The goal is to get a minimum of five hours uninterrupted sleep each night. To improve the quality of your sleep, don't look at your phone before going to bed, and sleep in a dark room.

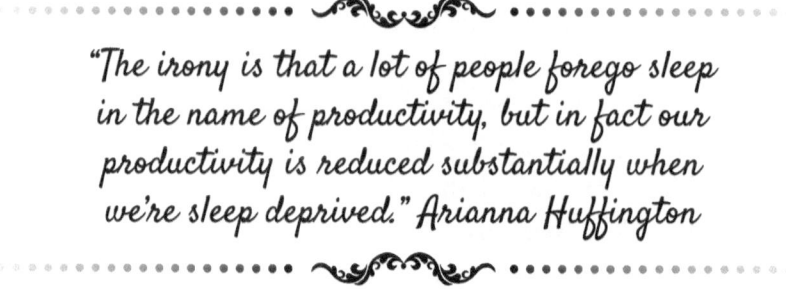

"The irony is that a lot of people forego sleep in the name of productivity, but in fact our productivity is reduced substantially when we're sleep deprived." Arianna Huffington

We know exercise is important to our health, and it's just as important to our productivity. A study found that employees who exercise regularly are 50% more productive than employees who only exercise occasionally.

improves muscle strength and boosts endurance. By delivering oxygen and nutrients to our tissues, it helps our cardiovascular system to work more efficiently. When our heart and lungs work more efficiently, we have more energy to get through the day.

To be productive, we need to make exercise a priority. For me, the turning point was once again in my mind. I changed my focus, and started thinking how exercise is an investment in my future. I can't 'wake up' when I am 60 years old and decide to look after my body. To be fit and fabulous at 60, I need to exercise and eat well today.

If you're not in the habit of exercising, start small. Aim for 20 minutes a day, and as your fitness improves you will find yourself wanting to do more. Rather than seeing exercise as a chore, find an activity you really enjoy. It also helps to make exercise a family affair. I would often use the excuse that going to the gym would take away time with my children. So, when I can, I combine family time and exercise.

When I have a goal, I am more motivated to exercise. I often enter 10 km or half marathons to motivate me.

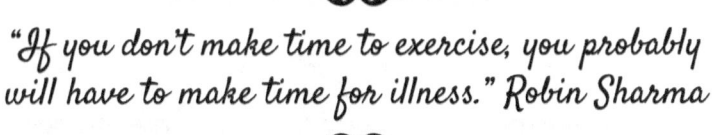

"If you don't make time to exercise, you probably will have to make time for illness." Robin Sharma

How to Manage Your Physical State – Summary

1. Eat for energy by choosing food by regularly eating whole grains, fruit and vegetables

2. Stay hydrated by drinking water throughout the day

3. Don't skip meals – aim for 3 healthy meals each day

4. Exercise daily

5. Get six hour of quality sleep each night

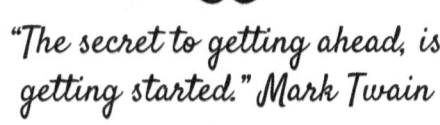

"The secret to getting ahead, is getting started." Mark Twain

PRODUCTIVITY IMPROVES WHEN YOU FOCUS ON ONE THING

Achievers operate differently. They have an eye for the essential. They pause just long enough to decide what matters and then allow what matters to drive their day." Gary Keller

Productive people know the importance of focusing on ONE thing. They know what their "Most Important Task" is and work on it with laser focus. They don't major in minor things. They are clear about their priorities and do whatever it takes to achieve their one thing.

But how do we know what our ONE thing is?

I am not sure if I believe we have *one* thing. It's more like *one thing right now*.

There are phases in our life, where we need to focus on one thing. There is a time to focus on career, then on kids, then perhaps on career again. It doesn't mean that the other areas of our life don't exist, but they're just not our ONE thing at that time.

I didn't achieve the results I wanted in my business or at home, because I wasn't focused. I was trying to do it all, and as a result, not doing anything very well. When we try to do too many things, it stops us from doing one thing really well… before we move onto doing something else really well. I'm learning to simplify my life and focus on what matters most.

How *do* you determine your one thing? Firstly, examine your stress. Where is it coming from? Could focusing your life reduce your stress? Revisit your personal values and your life vision. Is your life focused on achieving what's most important to you? What or who is distorting your focus?

Often financial stress can cause us to lose focus. It would have been easier to focus 100% on my children if I didn't have to work, but there are very few households that can rely on one income. When I fell pregnant with my first daughter, my husband and I were going through a very difficult time. The recession had seriously affected his industry and he had to close his business. We moved to a new city, but he couldn't find work. I was running my coaching practice, and considered finding full-time employment. I was 6 months pregnant at the time, and my job prospects were very slim. Fortunately, my husband found a job in another town, and when Sophia was 3 weeks old we moved to Johannesburg.

It was a very trying time for us, and we needed to get back on our feet quickly. During those first years of Sophia's life, I was simultaneously trying to be a good mother *and* build a successful business. My family has always been my most important thing, but during that time, I didn't focus on my daughter as much as I would have liked to.

As women, getting our finances in order often needs to be a priority so that we can look after those that matter most. The challenge is not getting caught up in the rat race or pursuing money to keep up with the Joneses.

It's only now – six years later – that I feel I can focus. I love what I do, and I still need to earn money, but my children need to be my ONE thing.

Focusing on your one thing is not a straight line, and the one thing is different for everyone. Consider if your life would be simpler, easier or better if you were more focused?

> *"Success comes down to this: being appropriate in the moments of your life." Gary Keller*

HOW TO FOCUS

1. Know Your ONE Thing Each Day

Often, we know what our one thing *in life* is, but the challenge is staying focused on your one thing during any respective day. Trying to do too much –even if those activities are in line with your purpose, personal values and life vision – can still lead to mediocre work or burnout. When it comes to planning and scheduling your days and weeks, always prioritise what's most important.

The Japanese have a saying, "When we go slow, we go faster". Slow down your life by focusing on one thing.

Gary Keller, entrepreneur, coach and author of *The One Thing*, said that when he focused his life (and those of his coaching clients), his (and their) results went through the roof.

I love this powerful question he asks himself every day, "What's the ONE thing I can do this week such that by doing it everything else would be easier or unnecessary?"

While planning and at the start of each day, ask yourself; what *must* I do to get closer to my vision? What task will have the biggest impact on reaching my goals? What one thing do I need to focus on to feel accomplished, satisfied or fulfilled?

We need to be doing fewer things for more effect instead of doing more things with side effects... Extraordinary results are directly determined by how narrow you make your focus." Gary Keller

2. Stop Multitasking

In the digital era, staying focused is becoming more of a challenge. Emails, notifications, messages and the telephone are just some of the digital distractions we face every day. Not to mention the external distractions, like our colleagues or kids; or the internal distractions, like worrying. It seems multitasking has become a necessity if we want to survive in the digital era.

However, multitasking is doing more harm than good. A study at the University of London found that people who multitasked experienced drops in their IQ, similar to a person who missed a night of sleep.

Multitasking gives us a false sense of accomplishment. We are busy, but at the end of the day, we have nothing to show for it.

Two things determine productivity and high-quality work: how much time we put into a task, and how focused we were during that time. By focusing on one thing at a time, we feel less stressed, and we'll do a better job.

There are times when we need to multitask. I multitask while doing mundane tasks such as running errands or making dinner. However, if I need to complete an important task, or I'm spending quality time with my family or friends, I turn off my phone and give them my full attention.

"You can do anything, but you can't do everything." Joe Duncan

3. Have a Healthy Brain

The topic of brain health is not as popular as body health. Besides controlling the functioning of our body, the brain is responsible for our thinking, decision making, problem-solving, creativity and emotional regulation (plus more). To be and stay focused, we need a healthy brain. Simply, a healthy brain equals a focused brain.

We can look after our brain by exercising. Besides being important to cardiovascular health, exercise stimulates various brain chemicals that leave us feeling happier and more relaxed. Exercise helps us sleep better, and quality sleep is essential to restoring and resting our brain.

Drinking water helps the brain perform optimally. Dehydration can cause problems with focus, memory, brain fatigue and brain fog, and much more. Water provides the brain the electrical energy it needs for all brain functions, including thought and memory.

According to Dr Corinne Allen, founder of the Advanced Learning and Development Institute, brain cells need twice as much energy than other cells in the body. Water provides this energy more effectively than any other substance. (Source: Water Benefits Health, *Water and Brain Function How to Improve Memory and Focus*, by Merlin Hearn and Nancy Hearn)

We all know that too much sugar is bad for our waistline, but more and more studies are proving that it's detrimental to brain health too. Researchers at UCLA found that a diet high in sugar limits learning and memory, by literally slowing down the brain. Some studies have proven that too much sugar can cause depression, dementia and could increase the risk of Alzheimer's disease. It's important to eat less sugar for long term brain health.

4. Take Regular Breaks

Taking regular breaks helps with focus. The human brain wasn't built for long hours of focus. Our brains are wired to constantly be on the lookout for changes in the environment and threats to our survival. We're not naturally wired to focus on one thing for a very long time. All we need is a quick break to help our brain refocus.

Breaks equal breakthroughs!

Have you ever had a light bulb moment in the shower? That's because breaks can result in breakthroughs!

Our brains have two modes: the "focused mode," which we use when we're learning, writing or working; and the "diffuse mode", when we're more relaxed. Scientists have proven that brain activity increases when our minds wander and this is the reason we often have breakthroughs while doing mundane tasks like taking a shower or driving.

There are many ways to implement the habit of taking breaks into your day. The Pomodoro Technique is a time management method developed by Francesco Cirillo, and made famous by his tomato timer ('tomato' is Pomodoro in Italian). Set a timer for 25-minutes and when it goes off, take a quick 5-minute break. Walk around the room, stretch your legs and have a glass of water.

Another method is to work for 90-minutes, then take a 15 minute or longer break. When a professor studied elite performers such as violinists, athletes, actors and chess players, he found that they practised for no more than 90 minutes at a time. This is a popular productivity technique, because it works with our bodies' natural rhythms. (Source: Fast Company, *Why You Need To Stop Thinking You Are Too Busy To Take Breaks*, Courtney Seiter).

5. Clear the Clutter to Focus

Clutter can be emotional and physical. It is difficult to focus when we have a lot on our mind. The best way to clear emotional clutter is to write things down in the form of to-do lists (which I write about later) and journaling.

I find that the process of writing down my emotions helps me to release how I am feeling and gives me the energy to move forward. Sometimes I want to purge how I feel and never read it again. I use a method called 'free-writing'. I write and write and write until I feel that I have nothing more to add. I don't read what I have written – I don't want to feel those emotions any longer or analyse them; I just want to release them and move forward. After I have finished writing, I tear up the page and throw it away.

Another method I use before a coaching appointment or even before a meeting, is "clearing the space". At the beginning of a coaching appointment I ask my client to briefly share, two or three things that are going on in the background that could prevent them from being focused in our meeting. They can't be long stories; just one sentence to describe a situation or event that is preoccupying their mind. After each statement, they need to label it with an emotion; then decide if they are able to put it aside and focus on the meeting.

For example, I am going for dinner tonight with friends. I am excited. I have a presentation later this afternoon. I am anxious.

The simple act of labelling an emotion calms the limbic system of the brain, the part of the brain responsible for emotional regulation, and enables us to focus.

Our focus can also be diluted by physical clutter. We recently sold our house and in preparation for our move I got rid of a lot of physical *stuff*; countless items that we had collected over the years that wouldn't necessarily serve us going forward. During the process, I realized how much we accumulate and how many things we hold onto (as a society), which often have no real value to us.

Similarly, on an emotional level, we chase ideals which, at the end of the day, don't really matter; and hold onto grudges, failures, disappointments and limiting beliefs that don't add value to our lives.

I discovered that by clearing physical space, there is room for new (and even better) things. When you clear your mind, you open up to new possibilities, adventures and meaning.

I understand that clearing clutter can be difficult. I can only speak from my experience and say that letting go helps you move forward. Releasing what you're holding onto, allows you to receive something new.

Marie Kondo, author of *The Life-Changing Magic of Tidying Up*, and advocate of the KonMari Method, the Japanese art of decluttering and organising, recommends tidying up all at once, as things get messy again quickly. She recommends that we visualise our ideal lifestyle and understand why we want to live that way. When clearing clutter, we need to determine if each item "sparks joy" and to only cherish what we love.

Her method recommends tidying by category, not location. If you are tackling your clothes, then you must get all the clothes out of every closet and drawer in every room first; and discard items, before you place things back.

How to Focus – Summary

1. Know your one thing each day

2. Stop multitasking

3. Have a healthy brain by exercising regularly, drinking water, and reducing sugar

4. Take regular breaks

5. Clear physical and emotional clutter

PRODUCTIVITY & TECHNOLOGY

One of the biggest challenges we face today is constant connectivity. Digital devices are with us wherever we go and we're constantly receiving messages and notifications. Even when we have a moment to spare, we instantly connect to social media. Constant connectivity is making it difficult to be present. It can distract us from our purpose, and our health and relationships can suffer, if we don't manage it effectively.

Technology has changed the way we work and live, and it's affecting our health. The structure of our brains hasn't changed since the days of the cave man, but today we are receiving a thousand times more stimuli than we did 10 000 years ago. One of the reasons we are experiencing more chronic stress than ever before, is because our brains can't cope with the information overload.

Disturbingly, technology is rewiring our brain… and not for the better. Our constant connectivity has resulted in shorter attention spans, plus a decline in memory and empathy. Humans are disconnecting; we have disturbed sleeping patterns; and social media addiction is a reality.

I am not against technology, in fact I love it. I love how I am able to stay connected with family and friends around the world, and how I am able to work from anywhere. To be productive, we need to have a balanced approach to how we use technology, and create healthy habits and boundaries for emailing, social media and the Internet.

EMAIL MANAGEMENT

According to a study by the McKinsey Global Institute, an average employee spends 13 hours a week reading and responding to email. That's 13 hours we could be spending on important projects, time with our kids, making a difference or having fun.

Emails are essential in business but we need to learn how to manage them effectively. Not only are we receiving too many emails, we have stopped connecting with our colleagues. Relationships are strained and misunderstandings happen because emails are written quickly, without consideration for tone and manners.

To effectively manage emails, we need to set boundaries and adopt positive habits. For me, changing when and how I check emails, has really helped. I don't check emails or social media when I wake up or first thing at the office. Mornings are the best time of the day to get things done; especially activities that require good-quality thinking. It's when the pre-fontal cortex (the part of the brain that we use for complex thinking) is most productive.

I don't check emails after hours – this is my time for family, fun or rest; or before I go to sleep. Exposure to the 'blue light' used on smartphones disrupts the production of melatonin, the hormone essential for sleep.

In the past, there would be days when I would do nothing else, except check emails. A perfect example of being busy, but unproductive. These days, I've limited the amount of time I spend checking emails.

Tim Ferris, author of *The 4 Hour Work Week*, suggests checking emails three times a day for 30 minutes at a time. He recommends setting up an auto-responder to inform people of the times you check email and to provide your mobile number for anything urgent.

Author Kevin Kruse interviewed over 200 ultra-successful people– including seven billionaires, 13 Olympians, and accomplished entrepreneurs – about productivity. One of the habits they had in common was that they only read their emails a few times a day, and they scheduled time to process their emails. For some, that is once a day; for others, it is morning, noon, and night.

I've suggested this habit in my time management workshops, and the audience usually erupts in laughter or rolls their eyes. Comments are made such as "That's impossible for the kind of work I do." Or "You don't understand - I need to be connected to email 24 hours a day!"

WHY HAVE EMAILS HAVE BECOME OUR HIGHEST PRIORITY?

In the workplace, we have created a dangerous culture around emails. People feel they are frowned upon if they don't reply immediately. There is an expectation to respond at all hours of the day and night. We spend more time emailing than talking; more time connected to the Internet than connecting with people. Emails should support our work, not be our work.

Another way I limit my time on emails, is by closing my Outlook when I am busy with other work. Notifications can be hard to resist, so I eliminate the temptation by turning off my notifications and removing email from my phone.

When it's time to check emails, I've adopted the habit of reading an email once and taking action immediately. Sometimes we wait until we're in the right mood and add it to our already full to-do list. I've found the easiest way to eliminate email overload is to read and respond immediately.

I use the 4 D's when it comes to reading and responding to emails – delete, do, delegate or divide.

DELETE – Spam, jokes or any time-wasting emails. If your inbox is inundated with unwanted mailers or blogs, take 10 seconds to unsubscribe. This will save you time in the future.

DO – If an email needs a response, and you're able to respond with the necessary information, don't wait for the right mood, do it immediately.

DELEGATE – If you need input from someone else or you're not the right person, delegate the email. Take time to clearly explain what is required, your desired outcome and the deadline. Ineffective delegation causes a lot of unnecessary stress and time wasting in the work place.

DIVIDE – Create folders in your inbox to organise your emails. I have a READ folder (for blogs and newsletters that I want to read – nothing important or urgent); an ACTION folder (for emails that require a follow up); and various other folders, such as Travel, Finances etc. An organised filing system saves a lot of time.

In an article written for Fast Company, Zach Hanlon, a sales and marketing expert recommends filing your emails by deadline. He advocates that your inbox is only for emails as they arrive. They shouldn't stay there any longer than it takes to file them into another folder. The exception to this rule is when you respond immediately and are waiting for an immediate response.

He recommends having a TODAY folder for everything that requires a response today. A THIS WEEK folder for everything that requires a response before the end of the week, and a THIS MONTH/QUARTER for everything that needs a longer-term response. Finally have a FYI folder for items that are informational. (Source: Fast Company, *The Only Five Email Folders Your Inbox Will Ever Need*, Zach Hanlon)

It's useful to ask colleagues to indicate when they need a response in all emails. This will help you prioritise the influx of emails and requests.

Social media is another daily distraction. I love social media because it connects me with family and friends around the world, but I can easily waste a couple of hours on Facebook without giving it much thought. Just like emails, we need to set boundaries for when and how we use social media. If your self-control is limited (like mine), there are Apps that restrict or limit your time on social media, or simply remove the various social media platforms from your devices.

"Most inboxes overflow with unimportant emails masquerading as priorities. Tackling these tasks in the order we receive them is behaving as if the squeaky wheel immediately deserves the grease." Gary Keller

IS IT TIME FOR A DIGITAL DETOX?

Kovert is a research organisation based in London and New York. Employees include neuroscientists, psychologists, and philosophers who design experiments to learn about how technology is changing people's bodies and behaviours.

In a recent study, they invited a group of 35 CEOs, entrepreneurs, and other influencers on a trip to Morocco to observe their behaviour with and without technology. They discovered after a few days without technology, participants had improved posture, deeper friendships, creative conversations, improved memory, more efficient sleep and new perspectives. (Source: Fast Company, *What Really Happens To Your Brain And Body During A Digital Detox*, Elizabeth Segran)

I am not suggesting that we give up social media all together. However, it may be beneficial to take mini digital detoxes each week or month. For two full days, such as Saturday and Sunday, don't go on social media or use any digital device. I've tried it, and I found that I more rested and relaxed come Monday morning.

"Be addicted to your passions, not your distractions."

How to Manage Your Email – Summary

1. Limit your time on email to three times a day

2. Don't read emails first thing in the morning or before you go to sleep

3. Turn off notifications on your desktop and phone

4. Apply the 4 D's – Delete, Do, Delegate, Divide

5. Implement a Digital Detox one day a week

TIME MANAGEMENT BASICS FOR PRODUCTIVITY

1. EFFECTIVE PLANNING

There's an old saying, "If you fail to plan, you plan to fail." Effective planning helps us focus and sets us up for the best possible day. Planning takes place in various stages – life plans, annual plans, quarterly plans, weekly plans and daily plans.

This might sound overwhelming, but a life plan is essentially your life vision. Annual plans and quarterly plans are created by your life vision and big projects. Weekly and daily plans are the steps you need to achieve your annual goals, projects and commitments.

Annual Plans

At the beginning of a year set three SMART goals that are in line with your Life Vision and Personal Values. I believe in focusing on three big goals, rather than five or six goals, which may dilute your focus.

Ask yourself, what do I need to do this year to get closer to fulfilling my life vision? What would I like to change, improve or learn this year? What would make this year truly amazing? What do I need to focus on? What will bring me closer to living out my personal values?

Write these goals down and keep them in a place where you will see them every day. I like to keep my goals in my journal, digitally on my desktop, and in my calendar. Jack Canfield, author of *The Success Principles* and one of my favourite personal development coaches, suggests writing your goals on 3 X 5 cards (speech cards), and keeping them in your purse.

The next step is to brainstorm everything you need to do to achieve your goals. Make a list of how you can achieve these goals, who can support you, what specific actions you need to take, and milestones you need to achieve your goals. Edit your list by selecting the best strategy and give each item a deadline.

Here's an example:

Annual Goal 1	I will run the Key West Half Marathon on 14 January 2018 in 2.5 hours.
Check In	Will this goal help me live out my personal values? Will it move me closer to my Life Vision?
Brainstorm	Buy running shoes. Register for race. Join a running club. Go to physiotherapist. Download a running programme. Follow running groups on social media. Get a personal trainer to assist with strength training. Swim to improve core and leg strength. Enter shorter races.
Plan	Buy running shoes by 1 March. Register for race immediately. Go to physiotherapist once a month. Research running programmes and download a programme by 1 March. Join a running club and run twice a week starting 1 April. Swim once a week to improve core and leg strength. Go to the gym once a week for strength building exercises.
Schedule	Take the items in your plan and schedule them in your calendar.
Milestones	Run 5kms (3 miles) by 1 June. Run 10 kms (6 miles) by 1 September. Run 16km (10 miles) by 1 November.

If you find an annual goal or project overwhelming, break it down into smaller more manageable tasks. If you want to write a book, break it down into quarterly plans. By the first quarter you will have completed your research. By the second quarter, you will have created an outline and structure. By the third quarter, you will have written your first draft. At the end of the final quarter, you will have an edited version ready to submit to a publisher.

2. TO-DO LISTS

To do or not to do – that is the question.

I believe that writing to-do lists is essential; not only for productivity, but also for being present. Our minds receive about 68 000 messages a day (80% of which were the same as yesterday) and writing down our thoughts helps our brain to cope. By writing things down, we are clearing the mind to focus on what's in front of us, and to identify our priorities. The reason most to-do lists never get done is because we use them as a brain dump, more than a focused, prioritised success list.

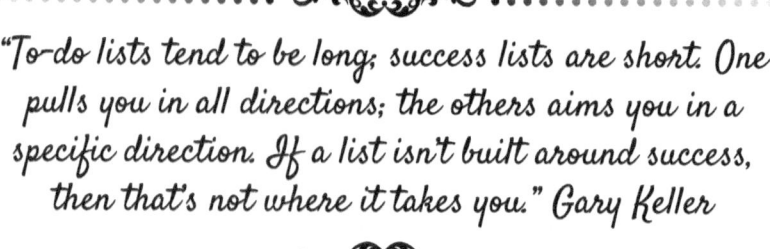

"To-do lists tend to be long; success lists are short. One pulls you in all directions; the others aims you in a specific direction. If a list isn't built around success, then that's not where it takes you." Gary Keller

For a to-do list to work it needs to be planned, prioritised and scheduled. The best way to use a to-do list is to write your list at the end of each day. Don't waste valuable time first thing in the morning writing a to-do list; instead, use this time to complete an important task. Your brain is at its most productive in the morning, so use this time for tasks that require complex thinking.

Writing your to-do list at the end of the work day helps you to switch off from work and focus on your loved ones. You don't have to worry about what's happening at work because you have a plan for the next day.

The next step is to look at your to-do list and identify your one thing. What's the ONE thing I can do this week that will make everything else easier or unnecessary. What *must* I do to get closer to my vision? What task will have the biggest impact on reaching my goals? What one thing do I need to focus on to feel accomplished, satisfied or fulfilled?

Your one thing needs to be scheduled, and the time remaining will determine how many items you can leave on your to-do list.

Keep your to-do list short. Look at the remaining items, and rank them in order of importance based on your priorities and deadlines. If you struggle to prioritise your to-do list, remember your Personal Values, Life Vision and Annual and Quarterly Goals. Knowing and understanding them helps determine what you need to do on a daily basis.

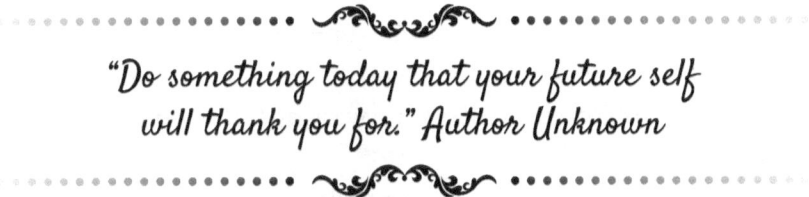

"Do something today that your future self will thank you for." Author Unknown

WHAT'S ON YOUR DON'T-DO LIST?

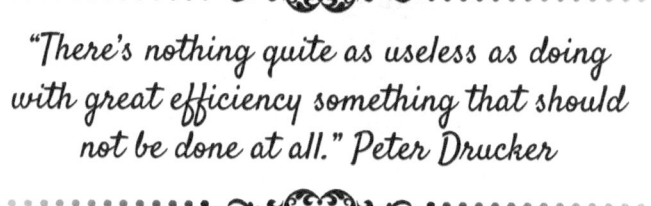

"There's nothing quite as useless as doing with great efficiency something that should not be done at all." Peter Drucker

What you DON'T do, gives you time to do what you *need* to do. Being clear and confident about what you don't do (and similarly what you don't want to do), eliminates time wasting indecision and helps you focus on your priorities.

This is what's on my don't-do list. I don't...

- Check emails first thing in the morning, after work hours or on weekends. If anyone needs me urgently, they can phone me.
- Browse social media while I'm with my kids or other people. Firstly, it's rude, and secondly, it's important to be present with the people who are present.
- Agree to meetings or social events before checking my calendar. I need to make sure that everything I do is in line with my priorities and values.
- Eat at my desk or in the car. I try to be mindful of what I am eating and enjoy my food.

Timothy Ferris, author of *The 4-Hour Work Week*, suggests that we don't answer phone calls from unrecognised numbers. They are an unwanted interruption and put you in a poor negotiating position. He recommends not agreeing to meetings or calls with no clear agenda or end time, and turning your phone off for one full day each week.

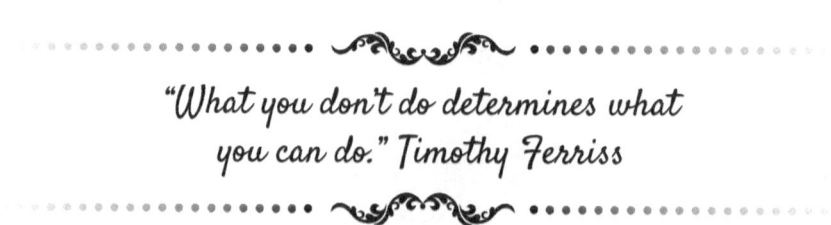

"What you don't do determines what you can do." Timothy Ferriss

3. SCHEDULING

"The secret of your success is found in your daily routine." John Maxwell

A to-do list often remains undone because it doesn't get scheduled. It lies on our desk or phone, and only gets looked at once or twice a day. Scheduling your to-do list in your calendar ensures that your tasks are top of mind.

A useful scheduling technique is Time Blocking, where you dedicate time to each task, starting with your one thing. Preferably schedule your one thing first thing in the morning, before emails, as your brain is most alert and focused at this time of the day.

Remember that breaks equal breakthroughs. Work in 25 to 90-minute increments and take breaks of 5 - 15 minutes before restarting your work.

"Either you run the day or the day runs you." Jim Rohn

4. PREPARATION & ORGANISATION

Being prepared and organised saves you time in the future. I've identified the areas of my work and life that can be prepped ahead of time, and automate, delegate and prepare as much as possible in advance.

At Home

There are times when I am feeling inspired and put on a spread that Nigella would be proud of. But more often than not, I find cooking a chore. It takes a lot of time and energy, which I don't usually have at the end of a day. So, when I am feeling inspired, I tend to cook and bake – a lot. I freeze meals for the nights when I don't feel like cooking, or for when something unexpected comes up, and have healthy snacks readily available. I often set a Sunday afternoon aside every three weeks to prepare meals and snacks for the weeks ahead.

As much as I can, I prepare for the next day, the night before. I pack bags and lay out school clothes, and make sure that I know what's on the agenda for the following day.

I am a morning person so I prefer getting up earlier than everyone else to make lunches, and spend some alone time before the day ahead.

The Office

I find having a neat desk and organised office space helps me get through a day calmly and efficiently. Taking a few extra minutes to file and label properly, can save you hours in the future.

I've wasted so much time in the past trying to remember digital passwords, that I now keep all my pins and passwords in one diary in one place. There's also a great app for this called Universal Password Manager.

Automation is possibly the most useful time saving technique in the office. I automate regular tasks as much as possible. Not only does this help save time, but it helps with planning. I schedule newsletters, blog posts and social media posts in advance, using the Mail Chimp automation and scheduling functions, Word Press to schedule posts, and Buffer for social media.

5. DECISION-MAKING

The need to make quick, quality decisions are an essential time management and career skill. We can waste a lot of time deciding what to do. When we procrastinate making a decision, it weighs us down and blurs our focus. Making quick, quality decisions saves time and energy.

To make quality decisions quickly, gather as much information as possible about your options. I find it useful to draw up a Pros and Cons list. What are the positives and negatives of each option?

If you need more input, ask the opinions of three trusted friends or colleagues. Don't ask too many people because all these opinions may confuse you further.

Once you have gathered all the information, take a break and stop thinking about the decision. Remember breaks often lead to breakthroughs!

If you need more than a 10-minute break, set a time and date to make the decision. It's amazing how useful and calming this step can be. Carry on with the rest of your day, and when the time comes, trust your gut and make the decision.

Remember: no decision is perfect. There is no certainty about any decision. Just believe that the decision you made at the time, was the right one.

6. SAYING 'NO'

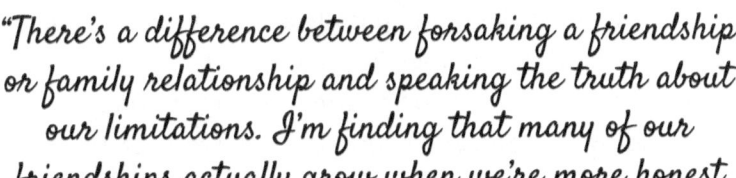

"There's a difference between forsaking a friendship or family relationship and speaking the truth about our limitations. I'm finding that many of our friendships actually grow when we're more honest about what we can and can't do." Shauna Niequist

'No' - This simple two-letter word causes a lot of unnecessary stress. Many of us, and especially women, don't like saying 'no'. When I think about saying 'no' I often worry what people will think. I am by nature a people pleaser, and don't like letting people down. But I've learnt that saying 'yes' – and subsequently not doing whatever it may be with energy, love and sincerity – is much worse than saying 'no'.

In the workplace, not saying 'no' can be detrimental to your career progression. People often take advantage of the 'yes girl' – and instead of being seen as someone who is always willing, you often get labelled as 'soft' or a 'pushover'.

It's important to be a helpful member of your team, but if you are constantly saying 'yes' to other people, there's a big chance that you are saying 'no' to your priorities.

Saying 'no', in other words being assertive, is acceptable. If we want to be more productive and present, we need to practice it more often.

The key is learning how to say 'no' in a way that makes us feel good about it. If we don't say 'no' assertively, we tend to come across as either aggressive or submissive.

An aggressive person doesn't consider the feelings of the other person and responds in a rude, sometimes sarcastic or even bullying manner. Whereas a submissive person finds it extremely difficult to say 'no'. They constantly make sacrifices for others, building resentment in the process.

It's important to be sincere when saying 'no', not to use tactics, but rather to be honest about your limitations. I find it helpful to not answer straight away. If I am unsure I can help, I ask for some time to look at my schedule and priorities, and honestly assess my capabilities.

If I can't help, it's time to say 'no' and stick to my decision. Saying 'no' with confidence is essential. Pay attention to your body language by sitting or standing up right, and maintaining eye contact. Communicate your reason with sincerity, making sure your tone of voice is calm yet assertive.

Always be polite, and if you can, offer solutions or alternatives. You may need to keep repeating your answer to get your point across. Repeat it calmly, nicely and firmly, and remind yourself that it's acceptable to say 'no'.

The following techniques are used by successful men and women around the world. Personal Development Coach, Sid Savara, suggests using the *Empathy Sandwich*, whereby we cushion a decline between two sincere and empathising comments. For example, "I am sure this must be very stressful for you. I would normally help, but I have to deliver this report by 3pm today. I'm sorry I don't have the time to help you today."

Eileen Carey, CEO of Glassbreakers, recommends saying 'no' when you are assigned a task that does not fall under your job description and could easily be accomplished by the person who is asking it. She believes that saying 'no' demonstrates your commitment to your role and the value of your time.

Johanna Lanus, CEO and founder of Work With Balance, keeps a list of long-term and short-term priorities and if a task or project doesn't fit into one of those buckets, 99% of the time she declines it.

Liz Wessel, CEO and cofounder of WayUp, says you don't always have to agree with every decision being made, but you should always feel empowered to question choices and, at the very least, to stir conversation. She affirms that asking why is a good substitute for saying 'no' because it forces the opposite side to explain and justify their point of view.

Alexandra Friedman and Jordana Kier, cofounders of LOLA, say 'no' to any meeting or project that does not directly or materially work toward the accomplishment of their key goals. They have a limited amount of time and resources, and it's their job to make sure that they're spending these resources on the highest-impact endeavours.

I've realized that successful people say 'no' all the time. Success is often not what we say 'yes' to, but what we say 'no' to.

> *"The difference between successful people and very successful people is that very successful people say 'no' to almost everything."* Warren Buffett

7. DELEGATION

Delegation is a necessary time management skill. We can't do it all, and we need other people to help us. The challenge is many of us don't like to delegate. I feel 'bad' asking for help because I don't like being a 'burden'. To overcome this, I've had to remind myself that I don't consider people who ask for my help a burden, so why would they consider me to be one. The key is asking the right people for help. People who you trust and who know you.

Another reason I don't like to delegate, and this one is more difficult to admit, is that I am not sure I will like how they do it. Deep down, I believe my way is better…

There are many ways to achieve something, and when I delegate I need to be open to the other person's approach. As long as the quality of the work or outcome is not compromised, we need to open ourselves up to doing things differently.

Do you like to delegate? What stops you from delegating? What do you believe about your colleagues or your family, that stops you from delegating?

The first step in delegating effectively is to choose the right person for the job. Make sure they have the necessary skills and knowledge to deliver the quality of work you require. Take the time to explain your request and the task in detail. Be clear about your expectations, and your time frame.

It's important to get agreement and commitment from the other person. Make sure they are willing and able to help you. And don't forget to offer your support and encouragement along the way.

Most importantly, if you have decided to delegate, then don't micromanage. Be flexible with your approach, but sure of your desired outcome. Finally, be thankful. Show your appreciation for their support.

8. MANAGING MEETINGS

Fortunately, as I work for myself, I don't have to deal with the overuse of meetings in the corporate world. Clients often complain that the biggest burden on their time is meetings. People love to have meetings for the sake of having a meeting. They're often held with no purpose and take us away from our one thing.

I believe if we changed the culture of meetings within organisations, we'd all be much more productive, effective and relaxed.

The first place to start is by examining the 'why'. Why are we having a meeting? What is the purpose? What is the desired outcome? What is the one thing we need to achieve in this meeting? By asking these questions, we will establish if the meeting is absolutely necessary.

If the meeting is necessary, then the next step is to decide who *must* be there – not who *should* be there, or who would be *nice* to have there. We need to decide whose input is 100% critical to the desired outcome of the meeting. Only invite these people. Don't waste anybody else's time, or invite people who may waste time in the meeting, giving information that is irrelevant or not useful.

If you are responsible for running the meeting, set an agenda and time frame, and email it to the participants beforehand. Arrive early and make sure the meeting venue is suitable and set up with the right equipment and refreshments.

At the start of the meeting set clear boundaries, such as a start and end time, and kindly request that no phones or laptops be used during the meeting. You may feel embarrassed or afraid to ask this, but remember that high quality work is only produced when we are 100% focused. If the desired outcome is clear, and your meeting is short (ideally meetings should not be longer than 30 - 45 minutes), then you are not offending anyone by requesting this.

At the end of the meeting, make sure everyone is clear on the next steps, and their role and responsibilities. Afterwards, it is a good idea to send out a short email summarising these points and including key outcomes and deadlines, so that any misunderstandings are avoided.

Famous entrepreneurs often have valuable insights into how to manage meetings. Richard Branson suggests having short meetings standing up, while Mark Cuban never takes meetings unless someone is writing a cheque.

How to Manage Your Time – Summary

1. Draft annual, quarterly and weekly plans

2. Write to-do lists at the end of each work day

3. Schedule your one thing and your to-do list

4. Be prepared and organised at home and in the office

5. Make quality decisions quickly

6. Learn to say 'no'

7. Delegate effectively

8. Have meetings that matter

PROCRASTINATION – THE ENEMY OF PRODUCTIVITY

"Every 'later' becomes a dream killer."

Do you fill your day with low priority tasks? Do you read emails several times without replying or doing anything with them? Do you sit down to start a high-priority task, and almost immediately go for a cup of coffee? Do you leave an item on your to-do list for a long time, even though you know it's important? Do you regularly say "yes" to unimportant tasks? Do you wait for the "right mood" or the "right time" to tackle the important task at hand?

If so, you may have a problem with procrastination. Don't despair because we all procrastinate to some degree, but if it's interfering with your results, then it's time to understand why you procrastinate.

We often procrastinate when we have too much to do. If I have too much on my plate, I put my head in the sand and avoid doing anything at all! A long to-do list can be overwhelming. We procrastinate because we don't know where to start.

The simplest way to overcome procrastination is to remind ourselves of our one thing. Our one thing always takes priority and should be done first. If we are procrastinating with our one thing, we may need to dig a little deeper to understand what is stopping us. Could it be fear?

The most challenging task on my to-do list is usually the one I avoid the most. I'm afraid of not knowing what to do and making a mistake. Fear is an emotion that stops us from taking action. But that's just it; it's just an emotion. There no truth in it; it's just a feeling.

In Feel the Fear and Do It Anyway, author Susan Jeffers says that the best way to overcome fear is to take action in spite of how you are feeling. The momentum you gain from taking the first step pushes you to do more. Break the item on your to-do list into smaller, less threatening steps. These small steps allow us to dip our toes, instead of diving in.

Sometimes we procrastinate when we have too much to do. This is why it's so important to say 'no' and to prioritise. By focusing on what's most important at work and at home, it removes the busyness from our lives and we feel less overwhelmed and stressed.

Conversely, we may procrastinate because we have too little to do. "I work well under pressure!" is an excuse I have used many times. There are times when I don't have much to do, and find that I don't have the motivation to do anything. I avoid what I can do and wait for the work to pile up before I actually do something.

Strangely, I do work well under pressure. I seem to be more focused and energised. The problem is if I use this excuse too often, the work piles up and I end up feeling overwhelmed, or deliver work that is less than my best.

If I find 'nothing' on my to-do list, I move the deadlines of certain projects. I change the due date so that I need to get it done sooner. This also gives me more time to work on it, if I am potentially not happy with the quality of the work.

Procrastination often occurs because we see no pleasure in doing it. Human beings are governed by a very simple principle – we do what brings us pleasure and we avoid what causes us pain. If we see exercise as something painful – something that is tiring, boring, pointless – then we won't do it. But if we link exercise to pleasure – something that brings us joy, strength, energy and vitality – then we do it.

Instead of focusing on the pain of doing the task, I focus on the pleasure. What are the benefits of doing it? Then I focus on the pain of NOT doing it. What are the consequences if I don't do it now? What will I miss out on? How could not doing it, impact my future? I link doing the task to very real, tangible pleasure and rewards.

Another useful way to overcome procrastination is to do the worst task first. Complete the item on your to-do list that you are dread the most, first thing in the morning. By getting it out of the way, you feel energised for the rest of the day and you don't have to carry the "weight" of it with you throughout the day. Another reason to do the worst task first is because our will power is highest in the morning. Think of self-control as a muscle; it gets tired after you use it. It's best to use this "muscle" first thing in the morning before fatigue sets in.

If procrastination is really a problem – get support. Ask a friend or colleague to hold you accountable, and agree on a consequence if you don't do it.

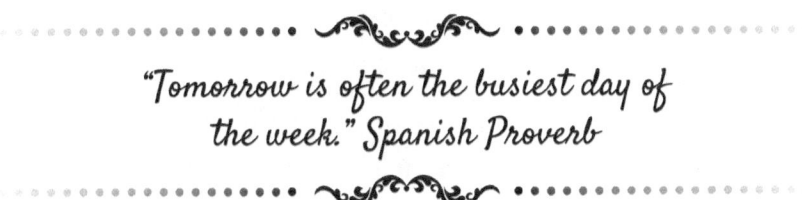

"Tomorrow is often the busiest day of the week." Spanish Proverb

WORK LIFE BALANCE

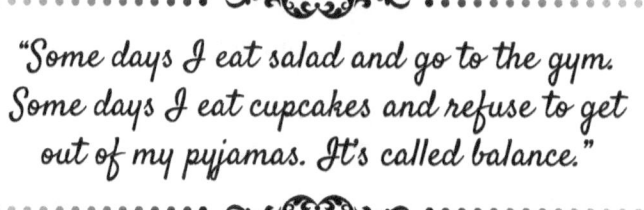

"Some days I eat salad and go to the gym. Some days I eat cupcakes and refuse to get out of my pyjamas. It's called balance."

Oprah once said, "We can have it all, but not all at once." It often feels that way when it comes to having a career and raising children. It feels like most of the time, when I am succeeding in one area, I am failing in the other.

For most women, our childbearing years and career-setting years coincide. I started my company at the end of 2008, I got married in 2009, had my first child in 2010, moved to a new city in 2011, and had my second child in 2014. All the while having grand expectations of success at work and at home.

I've had to redefine what success means to me, and part of this definition is work life balance.

For me, work life balance is more of a feeling than a goal. There are times when I need to prioritise one area over another, and that is okay. I just need to feel that I am trying my best. The lesson I've learnt in my short years of parenting, is that my kids don't want Super Mom. They want Mom who is happy. Mom who is loving. Mom who is there.

A study revealed that it's not how many hours parents spend with their children; instead, it is how engaged the parents are when they're with their children that is the most important factor. Being present wherever I am, and with whoever is there, helps me to feel balanced, and this requires being practical.

I've shifted from multitasking mamma to single-tasking mamma. When I am with my kids, I put my phone away and only check emails or social media when they are not around or have gone to bed. There is a growing concern about screen time for children. We can't expect our kids to disconnect if we aren't willing to. Setting digital boundaries is important if we want a balanced and productive life. We need time to switch off and focus on the people who are right in front of us.

If you struggle to switch off, remove tempting apps from your phone, or install apps that limit your time on social media and the Internet. Charge your phone away from family areas and make a rule that no-one is allowed to be on their phone at certain times of the day, such as meal times.

Preparation and planning create a happy and calm home. As mentioned before I try to prepare meals in advance and cook extra meals for freezing. I like to get up earlier than everyone else so I can pack lunches and have the household ready before the morning madness.

It's useful to keep one calendar so as not to miss important events. Diarise regular commitments and keep a family calendar and chalk board in the kitchen.

Work-life balance is possible if you get everyone involved. Balance is not just for you, it's for your family too. A healthy and happy mom makes a healthy and happy home. Ask for support from your partner, extended family and older children. Delegate and share the workload.

Take a break and don't work every weekend. You need time for family, friends and fun. Make your home life a priority. If your home life is a mess, you will never be happy at work.

Lastly, don't aim for perfection. If we look at balance as an even split, then it's never going to happen. There are times when we need to be more focused on work, than at home; and vice versa. My advice is that if you are constantly feeling out of balance, then you are neglecting your highest priorities – and something needs to change.

"To me, there are only a few important things. My health, having good relationships, and that's about it. It's pretty easy to balance that. We spend too much time balancing things we don't need in our lives. That turns our life into a circus act." Darius Foroux, Productivity Coach

PRESENT – Experience the Joy of Pressing Pause

I once read a story about a social experiment organised by the Washington Post. Its purpose was to examine perception, taste and priorities of people.

A man sat at a Metro station in Washington, D.C. and started to play the violin; it was a cold January morning. He played six Bach pieces for about 45 minutes. During that time, since it was rush hour, it was calculated that thousands of people went through the station, most of them on their way to work. Three minutes went by and a middle-aged man noticed that there was musician playing. He slowed his pace and stopped for a few seconds and then hurried on to meet his schedule.

A minute later, the violinist received his first dollar tip: a woman threw the money into his violin case and without stopping, continued to walk. A few minutes later, someone leaned against the wall to listen to him, but the man looked at his watch and started to walk again. Clearly, he was late for work.

The one who paid the most attention was a 3-year-old boy. His mother tagged him along, hurried but the kid stopped to look at the violinist. Finally, the mother pushed hard and the child continued to walk, turning his head all the time. This action was repeated by several other children. All the parents, without exception, forced them to move on.

In the 45 minutes the musician played, only six people stopped and stayed for a while. About 20 people gave him money but continued to walk their normal pace. He collected $32. When he finished playing and silence took over, no one noticed it. No one applauded, nor was there any recognition.

No one knew this, but the violinist was Joshua Bell, one of the best musicians in the world. He played one of the most intricate pieces ever written with violin worth 3.5 million dollars. Two days before his playing in the subway, Joshua Bell sold out at a theatre in Boston, where the seats averaged $100.

This is a real story. But remember, Joshua Bell playing incognito in the Metro station was organised by the Washington Post as part of a social experiment about perception, taste and priorities of people. The outlines were based on a commonplace environment at an inappropriate hour; from there, certain questions were asked. Do we perceive beauty? Do we stop to appreciate it? Do we recognise the talent in an unexpected context?

One of the possible conclusions from this experience could be: if we do not have a moment to stop and listen to one of the best musicians in the world playing the best music ever written, how many other things are we missing?

"In the age of constant movement, nothing is as urgent as sitting still." Pico Iyer

MINDFULNESS – A PRACTICAL WAY TO PRESS PAUSE

"Wherever you are, be all there."

It's easy to get caught up in our daily routine, rushing from one place to the next, not focusing or appreciating the moment. Practising mindfulness helps us to be present and peaceful, regardless of what is going on around us.

Mindfulness is an awareness of the present moment. It's the ability to slow down our lives and notice our thoughts, feelings, and our surroundings, with curiosity rather than judgement.

Researchers have proved that practising mindfulness has many benefits. It improves focus, memory and patience, and increases feelings of well-being and calmness. Mindfulness delays the ageing brain, reduces muscle tension, and improves cardiovascular health and circulation.

In the 21st century, digital communication and the demands of everyday life, make mindfulness a challenge. Mindfulness becomes easier when it's a habit, and I've added small steps to my daily routine to make me more mindful.

I start my day by getting up early to read and pray, which allows me to start my day more mindfully. When I exercise, I incorporate yoga stretches and deep breathing, which enhances the feeling of mindfulness. And throughout the day, I take occasional mindful pauses to notice my surroundings, gather my thoughts and appreciate the moment.

Try a mindful pause right now. Close your eyes and take three deep breaths. When you take a deep breath, ensure that your shoulders don't move; instead, expand your lower chest and abdomen. Think of your body as a balloon that swells up as air enters it. Thereafter open your eyes and notice your surroundings with all your senses. What do you see, smell, taste, hear and feel? How does your body feel? Appreciate the moment.

I practise this mini-mindful pause whenever I feel stressed. It helps me to centre and refocus.

Practising mindfulness as a parent has helped me to be more present. There's the old saying that children want our presence not our presents. There are times that it's okay to be distracted, but children are lot more perceptive that we give them credit for. They know when we aren't "really there" and they appreciate it so much when we are.

> "Sink deeply into the world as it stands. Breathe in the smell of rain and the scuff of leaves as they escape across the driveways on windy nights. This is where life is, not some imaginary, photo-shopped dreamland. Here. Now. You, just as you are. ME, just as I am. The world, just as it is. This is the good stuff. This is the best stuff there is." Shauna Niequist

Pause for Personal Growth

"Who looks outside dreams. Who looks inside awakens." Carl Jung

Life is a journey of learning. We're constantly learning about others, the world and ourselves. However, personal growth is not something we tend to prioritise until there is a crisis. It was only when I was unhappy in my career that I decided to learn about myself, and think consciously about who I was. I am grateful for that crisis because it introduced me to a world that has encouraged, inspired, educated and challenged me.

I want to encourage you not to wait for a crisis. Personal growth is not a time-consuming activity. It's a time-enhancing activity. When we know ourselves better, we know what to focus on, what to stop, what to grow, and we appreciate ourselves, the people around us, and the moment much more.

The mind is like an elastic band. Once stretched it cannot return to its original size. Reading expands the mind, and has been one of the greatest sources of my personal growth. I have read hundreds of books that have helped me grow spiritually, emotionally, physically, financially and intellectually.

They say that nothing beats experience. Our failures can be a source of personal growth if we pause long enough to learn from them.

Taking time to reflect, think and journal, grows our compassion and understanding, for ourselves and others.

No one's journey through life is perfect. The weight of trauma, unforgiveness and anger will weigh you down and it becomes impossible to move forward. Getting support for the difficult experiences you have faced is important to your personal growth.

"People are anxious to improve their circumstances but are unwilling to improve themselves. They therefore remain bound." James Allen

Pause for Yourself

"You're going to get tired while pursuing your dreams. You need to rest, not quit." Katrina Kavvolos

Putting yourself last on your to-do list will stop you from being purposeful, productive and present. 'Me-time' should be a priority, instead of a maybe.

I love the announcement the flight attendant makes before take-off. "In the event of an emergency, place your oxygen mask on yourself first, before helping the person next to you."

There's a valuable lesson hidden in that announcement. We need to look after ourselves so that we can look after others. We need to prioritise our physical and emotional health so that we have the energy, focus and compassion to look after others.

In the past, I made the excuse that I don't have time to exercise because I need to spend time with my children. This is short sighted – if I sacrifice my health (by not exercising, eating correctly or resting) then one day I may not be there for them at all.

Even if you don't have children, your dreams require energy. You need to prioritise your physical and emotional health, to achieve them.

When we take care of ourselves, we confirm our worth. When we give to ourselves (whether it's the gift of me-time, rest, love or acknowledgement), we have more to give to others.

Pause each day for yourself. Make time to exercise, reflect on your life vision, and assess (and allow for) personal growth. Remember to have fun and enjoy life. Do the things that bring you joy and make time to de-stress and unwind.

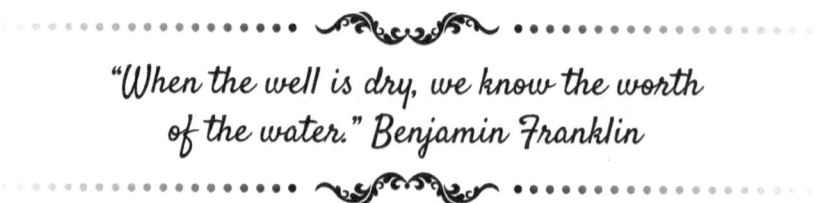

"When the well is dry, we know the worth of the water." Benjamin Franklin

Conclusion

"Be still and know that I am God." Psalm 46:10

Over the years I have blogged about my life and career. Looking back, it was a weekly practice of pressing pause. Writing helped me to reflect and learn. I laugh and cringe at some of my earlier blogs, but I understand it was all part of my learning, and this practice has helped me to press pause again.

I have pressed pause to embark on a new adventure. Pausing has helped me take this next step with purpose. I have a vision, but unlike a few years ago, I am not holding onto to it so tightly that I suffocate myself and others, in its pursuit.

Pausing has allowed me to treat myself with more compassion and less judgment. And when we treat ourselves better, we are able to treat those around us better too. I am more present – more conscious of what is important in life – and pressing pause revealed that to me.

I once read that time is the great equaliser. Some of us have more time on earth, but we are all given 24 hours in a day. What you do with those hours is up to you.

Have a purpose, but don't pursue it at all costs. Realise what's most important and hold onto that, no matter the cost. Be productive, but not at the expense of others or your health. Health is wealth; without it, we have nothing. Be present. Pause and notice where you are and who you are with. If you don't like what you see, have the courage to press pause and change it.

> *"It's not only moving that creates new starting points. Sometimes all it takes is a subtle shift in perspective, an opening of the mind, an intentional pause and reset... to start to see new options and new possibilities." Kristin Armstrong*

Resources & Recommended Reading

I have read hundreds of books on the subjects of personal development, time management, business and career success. My philosophy and ideas have no doubt been influenced by these books.

While writing my book, I have tried to credit authors when I have quoted directly from a source, and I have included a list of recommended reading to acknowledge any books that may have inspired this book directly or indirectly. These books have shaped me and no doubt this book. In addition, I have listed articles I have read as part of my research.

Internet Resources

Barker, Eric; *6 Things the Most Organized People Do Every Day*, Motto. Time.com, Time Magazine, 26 February 2016

Bradberry, Travis; *14 Things Ridiculously Successful People Do Every Day*, Entrepreneur.com, Entrepreneur Magazine, 3 June 2016

Bradberry, Travis; *How Smart People Work Less and Get More Done*, Entrepreneur.com, Entrepreneur Magazine, 4 April 2017

Fell, Jason; *5 Steps to Organizing Your Life and Doing Great Things This Year*, Entrepreneur.com, Entrepreneur Magazine, 9 January 2017

Ferriss, Tim; *The Not-To-Do List: 9 Habits to Stop Now*, Tim.Blog, Timothy Ferriss, 2017

Foroux, Darius; *Why I Don't Believe In Work-Life Balance*, DariusForoux.com, 20 October 2016

Grothaus, Michael; *Workers need one hour of activity to counter every 8 hours at a desk*, Fast Company.com, Fast Company Magazine, 28 July 2016

Hanlon, Zach; *The Only Five Email Folders Your Inbox Will Ever Need*, Fast Company.com, Fast Company Magazine, 9 January 2017

Hearn, Merlin, and Hearn, Nancy; *Water and Brain Function: How to Improve Memory and Focus*, WaterBenefitsHealth.com, Water Benefits Health, 2017

Kreider, Tim; *The 'Busy' Trap*, Opinionator.blogs.nytimes.com, New York Times, 30 June 2012

Lindzon, Jared; *Study Finds Work-Life Balance Could Be A Matter Of Life And Death*, FastCompany.com, Fast Company Magazine, 20 October 2016

Loria, Kevin, and Gould, Skye, *How smartphone light affects your brain and body*, BusinessInsider.com, Business Insider Magazine, 2 November 2016

Markman, Art; *How Writing To-Do Lists Helps Your Brain (Whether Or Not You Finish Them)*, FastCompany.com, Fast Company Magazine, 5 September 2016

Northrup, Christiane; *7 Tips To Organize Your Home Using the KonMari Method*, DrNorthrup.com, Dr Christiane Northrup, 2017

Ohio State University, *Body Posture Affects Confidence In Your Own Thoughts*, Study Finds, ScienceDaily.com, Science Daily, 5 October 2009

Rampton, John; *7 Reorganizational Strategies for Work and Life*, Entrepreneur.com, Entrepreneur Magazine, 1 December 2015

Segran, Elizabeth; *What Really Happens To Your Brain And Body During A Digital Detox*, FastCompany.com, Fast Company Magazine, 30 July 2015

Seiter, Courtney; *Why You Need To Stop Thinking You Are Too Busy To Take Breaks*, FastCompany.com, Fast Company Magazine, 2 September 2014

Wademan Dowling, Daisy; Balancing Parenting and Work Stress: A Guide, HBR.org, Harvard Business Review, 9 March 2017

Book Resources & Recommended Reading

Anthony Robbins (1991), *Awaken the Giant Within: How to take immediate control of your mental, emotional, physical & financial destiny*, New York, NY: Simon and Schuster

Arianna Huffington (2016), *The Sleep Revolution: Transforming Your Life, One Night at a Time*, New York, NY: Harmony Books

Dr Caroline Leaf (2013), *Switch On Your Brain: The Key to Peak Happiness, Thinking, and Health*, Grand Rapids, MI: Baker Books

Gary Keller & Jay Papasan (2013), *The One Thing: The surprisingly simple truth behind extraordinary results*, Austin, TX: Bard Press

Jack Canfield and Janet Switzer (2006), *The Success Principles(TM): How to Get from Where You Are to Where You Want to Be*, New York, NY: Harper Collins Publishers

Marcus Buckingham (2009), *Find Your Strongest Life: What the Happiest and Most Successful Women Do Differently*, Nashville, TN: Thomas Nelson

Shauna Niequist (2016), *Present Over Perfect: Leaving Behind Frantic for a Simpler, More Soulful Way of Living*, Grand Rapids, MI: Zondervan

Shefali Tsabury (2010), *The Conscious Parent: Transforming Ourselves, Empowering Our Children*, London, UK: Hodder Publishing

Timothy Ferriss (2007), *The 4-Hour Workweek: Escape 9-5, Live Anywhere, and Join the New Rich*, New York, NY: Crown Publishing

www.ingramcontent.com/pod-product-compliance
Lightning Source LLC
Chambersburg PA
CBHW031437210526
45464CB00005B/2235